CATS'
Miscellany

Lesley O'Mara

MICHAEL O'MARA BOOKS LIMITED

First published in Great Britain in 2005 by
Michael O'Mara Books Limited
9 Lion Yard, Tremadoc Road
London sw4 7nq

A CIP catalogue record for this book is available
from the British Library

The author and publisher are grateful to the following people:
William Geldart, for the use of his illustrations, Lesley Fotherby,
also for illustrations, and Athene Chanter and Sarah Jones for help
with assembling the text.

Illustrations on pages: title page, 7, 15, 25, 38, 40, 52, 68, 124
© William Geldart

Illustrations on pages: 8, 11, 41, 49, 51, 122 © Lesley Fotherby.
Courtesy of Chris Beetles Ltd, St James's, London

Illustration on page 44 by Edward Lear (1812–88),
Private Collection/Bridgeman Art Library

ISBN 978-1-84317-149-2

5 7 9 10 8 6 4

www.mombooks.com

Designed and typeset by Martin Bristow
Printed and bound in Finland by WS Bookwell, Juva

Contents

Ten Reasons Why You Have to Own a Cat   7

Cat Lovers   8

Cat Ancestors   9

It's a Cat's World – 1   9

Some Cat Breed Facts   11

Cats' Bodies   12

Cats on Postage Stamps   13

Some Exotic Female Cat Names   14

Some Exotic Male Cat Names   14

Cats' Whiskers   15

The White Cat   16

Cat Trouble   16

Psychic Cats?   18

Cats' Incredible Journeys – 1   18

Cats' Food   20

Famous Cat Owners – 1   22

Purring   25

Cats' Ears   26

Top Cats   26

Cats' Chat   28

Moody Cats   29

Cat Naps   29

More Cats   30

Cats Versus Dogs   30

Contents

Cats and Milk	32
Having Kittens	32
Some Cat Behaviours	34
Cats' Curiosity	35
Some Cat Care	36
Cats' Eyes	37
How to Litter Train Your Cat	39
To Bath, or Not to Bath	39
Cat Fun	39
Hazardous Plants	41
Some Plants Poisonous to Cats – 1	41
Cat and Mouse	42
Famous Cat Owners – 2	42
Some Male Cat Names	46
Catty!	47
Not for the Squeamish	47
Getting Rid of Fleas	48
Catnip	49
Photographing Your Cat	50
Catty Problems Solved	52
Cat Versus Humans	54
Some Famous Cats	56
Cats' Legs and Paws	58
Cats in High Office	59
Some Plants Poisonous to Cats – 2	64
Celebrity Cats	64
Cat Legends	66

Contents

It's a Cat's World – 2	68
Cats' Skin and Fur	70
Cat Myths	70
Some Cat Luck and Lore	72
Some More Cat History	73
Nine Lives	76
The Black Cat	76
Cats' Blood	77
Each Nation to its Own – Cat Superstitions	77
More Lore – Cats and the Weather	79
Record-breaking Cats	80
Cats' Noses	82
Some Plants Poisonous to Cats – 3	83
Miscellaneous Cat Facts	83
Everlasting Cats	85
Cat Ages	85
Cats and Computers	86
How to Befriend a Cat	86
Famous Cat Owners – 3	87
Some Symptoms of a Poisoned Cat	91
Famous Ailurophobes	92
Cats in Art	92
Fat Cat – How to Tell if Your Cat is Overweight	96
Cats in Ancient Egypt	97
A Few Cat Dangers	98
Cats in Advertising	98
Cats and Music	99

Contents

Cats' Mouths	100
Believe It or Not	101
Inventions for Cats	102
Cats' Tails	103
A Great Mouser	104
Cats and Birds	104
Cats' Incredible Journeys – 2	106
What to do in a Cat Emergency	106
Cats at War	107
Cat Tricks	110
American Cat Laws	111
How to Toilet Train Your Cat	111
Great Heights	112
A Cat Hotel	112
The World According to Cats	113
Some Famous Cat Owners – 4	115
Other Cat Colours	118
It's a Cat's World – 3	118
Louis Wain	120
Cat Names	121
Some Female Cat Names	121
Some Plants Poisonous to Cats – 4	122
Chit C(h)at	123
Contrary Cats	124
How to Draw a Cat	124
Cats in Trees	124
Tail Piece	126

TEN REASONS
WHY YOU HAVE TO OWN A CAT

* Cats are always interested in whatever you are interested in.

* Cats never criticize.

* Cats don't mind what you watch on TV.

* Cats never need a babysitter.

* You never have to get up at 2 A.M. to feed a cat.

* Cats don't talk back.

* It's easy to make dinner for a cat.

* Cats don't need to be walked.

* Cats don't run up huge telephone bills.

* Cats don't mind if you call them silly names.

Cat Lovers

The smallest feline is a masterpiece. – Leonardo da Vinci

There are two means of refuge from the miseries of life: music and cats. – Albert Schweitzer

Time spent with cats is never wasted. – Colette

The cat has too much spirit to have no heart. – Ernest Menaul

No Heaven will not ever Heaven be
Unless my cats are there to welcome me.
Anonymous

I love cats because I enjoy my home; and little by little, they become its visible soul. – Jean Cocteau

There are no ordinary cats. – Colette

Never underestimate the power of a purr. – Anonymous

Cat Ancestors

No one knows exactly when or how the cat first appeared on earth. Most agree, however, that the cat's most ancient ancestor was almost certainly a weasel-like animal called *Miacis*, which lived between forty to fifty million years ago.

Miacis is believed by many to be the common ancestor of all land-dwelling carnivores, dogs as well as cats. But evidence suggests that the first cat appeared millions of years before the first dog.

Perhaps best known of the prehistoric cats is *Smilodon*, the sabre-toothed cat sometimes called a sabre-toothed tiger. This formidable animal hunted throughout much of the world but became extinct long ago.

It's a Cat's World – 1

Way down deep, we're all motivated by the same urges.
Cats have the courage to live by them. – Jim Davis

Cats are a mysterious kind of folk. There is more passing
in their minds than we are aware of. – Sir Walter Scott

Kittens are born with their eyes shut. They open them in about
six days, take a look around, then close them again for the better
part of their lives. – Stephen Baker

A cat has nine lives. For three he plays, for three he strays,
and for the last three he stays.
AN AMERICAN AND ENGLISH PROVERB

The cat is, above all things, a dramatist. – MARGARET BENSON

Children and cats in Venice learn to swim almost as soon
as they learn to walk. – JOAN AIKEN

Every waking moment was precious to her; in it she would find
something useful to do – and if she ran out of material and
couldn't find anything else to do she would have kittens.
MARK TWAIN, *on his cat, Sour Mash*

No matter how much cats fight, there always seems to be plenty
of kittens. – ABRAHAM LINCOLN

Cats are intended to teach us that not everything in nature
has a function. – GARRISON KEILLOR

Confront a child, a puppy, and a kitten with a sudden danger;
the child will turn instinctively for assistance, the puppy will
grovel in abject submission, the kitten will brace its tiny body
for a frantic resistance. – SAKI

SOME CAT BREED FACTS

✳ Non-pedigree cats are often more robust than cats that have been selectively bred.

✳ The ancestor of all domestic cats is the African wild cat, which still exists today.

✳ Today there are approximately one hundred distinct breeds of the domestic cat.

✳ The biggest breeds of cat are the Ragdoll and the Maine Coon breeds, and both can weigh 20 pounds (9 kilograms) or more. The smallest breed, the Singapura, can be five times smaller than the Ragdoll and Maine Coon.

✳ In the US, the Persian is the most popular breed of cat among homeowners, followed by the Siamese and the Maine Coon.

✳ The Havana Brown breed is so called because of its resemblance to the colour of Havana tobacco.

CATS' BODIES

The cat species can vary widely in size, but domestic cat breeds are among the smallest in the cat family. The average domestic cat measures between 8 to 10 inches (20 to 25 centimetres) high, and from the tip of the nose to the base of the tail is approximately 20 inches (51 centimetres) long. The tail itself is usually no longer than 15 inches (38 centimetres). Males are predictably heavier than females – around 15 pounds (6.8 kilograms) compared to 10 pounds (4.5 kilograms), though this can depend on skeletal size, and the amount of feeding by doting owners!

A cat's brain is closer in composition to a human's brain than that of a dog. The region of the brain responsible for emotion is located in the same place in both the human and the cat brain.

Lacking a true collarbone, a cat can squeeze its body through any space or gap into which it can fit its head. Feline whiskers act as feelers and allow the cat to judge whether they are likely to fit.

The flexibility of a cat's spine is the key to its remarkable physical versatility. The spine can be compressed to afford them comfort and sleep in snug places, or elongated to enable them to leap further.

While this will come as no surprise to cat owners who have been licked by their loving pets, cats lose as much fluid during self-grooming (through saliva) as they do through urinating.

The tongue of a domestic cat feels not too dissimilar to sandpaper, while the tongue of a big wild cat, such as the lion or

the tiger, is much rougher. This roughness serves several purposes – not only does it makes cleaning and grooming more effective, but also, in the wild, it serves as an effective tool to strip flesh from the bones of prey.

All cats – both domestic and wild – can purr. The volume of the purr can vary significantly, and can be so soft as to be inaudible to the human ear. Purring may begin as soon as a couple of days after birth. The purring sound is made by the cat vibrating its vocal cords in the voice box, but no one knows exactly how the cat uses these to produce purring, or why no other animal purrs.

A cat's litheness and grace are never-ending sources of pleasure and amazement to their owners. Its range of movements seem unlimited, whether rolling up into a ball, doubling-up sideways, stretching its back into practically a straight line, or arching its spine until front and back legs are only a few inches apart. It is no problem for a cat to turn its head backwards to allow its tongue to reach the fur on the centre of its back while grooming.

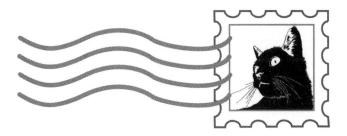

Cats on Postage Stamps

Across the world the postage stamp is often used to commemorate special occasions, honour the achievements of individuals, and mark the anniversaries of inventions, discoveries, and wars, among many other things. From Singapore to the Faeroe Islands, and from Gambia to Norway, there are thousands of stamps featuring cats – the first to appear was in Germany in 1887, and featured a cat with a fish in its mouth.

Other miscellaneous cat stamps include a Taiwanese stamp featuring the ginger cat Crookshanks from the Harry Potter novels, a US stamp celebrating the anniversary of the birth of Dr Seuss with a portrait of him along with his *Cat in the Hat* characters, and a British set illustrating the Rudyard Kipling *Just So Story*, 'The Cat That Walked By Himself'.

There is a Spanish stamp that commemorates aviator Charles Lindbergh's record-breaking flight from New York to Paris in May 1927, which portrays his cat, Patsy, watching Lindbergh's aeroplane take off. Pasty often accompanied Lindbergh on his flights, but did not go on the 1927 flight that made him famous.

SOME EXOTIC FEMALE CAT NAMES

Aida	Jasmin	Nuala	Saskia
Blanche	Jezebel	Paloma	Sapphire
Calypso	Minette	Pandora	Suki
Desdemona	Mitzy	Salambo	Topaz
Emerald	Mitsouko	Samsara	Yaki
Esmeralda	Nikita		Yoko

SOME EXOTIC MALE CAT NAMES

Boris	Dante	Micetto	Siam
Bruno	Farouk	Minou	Simba
Chilli	Fernando	Mufasa	
Claude	Milo	Orlando	

CATS' WHISKERS

The average cat has a total of twenty-four whiskers, arranged in four rows of three whiskers on either side of the face. The upper rows can move independently of the bottom rows.

Whiskers are more than twice as thick as ordinary hairs, and their roots are set three times as deep – they are closely connected to the nervous system. They are full of nerve endings which provide the cat with detailed information about air movement and pressure, as well as feedback on its surroundings. However, damage to a cat's whiskers may provoke discomfort, confusion or disorientation.

Further small groupings of whiskers are also situated on other parts of a cat's body, including above each eye and on the backs of the front paws.

The technical word for whiskers is *vibrissae*, which suggests their sensitivity to vibrations in air currents. Whiskers are also a tool for hunting, providing cats with vital information about the shape and movement of their prey.

Food bowls that are too small to accommodate a cat's head without its whiskers touching the sides can be an irritant, as the whiskers provide distracting and unwanted sensations to the cat. A cat's whiskers are another indicator of mood. Whiskers pointing forward signify curiosity; when pointing backwards the cat may feel nervous or threatened.

THE WHITE CAT

American superstition says that it is bad luck to see a white cat at night, but that dreaming of a white cat brings good luck.

If a white cat comes to your house it will bring with it good luck, provided that it stays.

CAT TROUBLE

Apparently, through scientific research, it has been determined that a cat's affection gland is stimulated by snoring, thus explaining my cat's uncontrollable urge to rub against my face at 2 A.M. – TERRI L. HANEY

Cats can be very funny, and have the oddest ways of showing they're glad to see you. Rudimace always peed in our shoes. W. H. AUDEN

A cat will wait until you've read your morning paper before tearing it to shreds. – ANONYMOUS

You must set down all the rules to your cat at the beginning of your relationship. You cannot add rules as you go along. Once these rules are set, you must never, under any circumstances, break any of them. Dare to break a rule, and you will never live it down. Trust me. – KATHY YOUNG

Garfield's Law: cats instinctively know the precise moment
their owners will awaken . . . then they awaken them
ten minutes sooner. – JIM DAVIS

The problem with cats is that they get the exact same look
on their face whether they see a moth or an axe-murderer.
PAULA POUNDSTONE

How do cats decide when to jump suddenly up from where they
were sitting comfortably, curled up, and dash madly around the
room, knocking over everything they encounter?
ANDREW KOENIG

Cats have an infallible understanding of total concentration –
and get between you and it. – ARTHUR BRIDGES

There is no snooze button on a cat who wants breakfast.
ANONYMOUS

When I played in the sandbox, the cat kept covering me up.
RODNEY DANGERFIELD

Cats may sense early on that you don't like paw prints on your
butter, but they will jump on to any surface in the home as long
as no one sees it happen. – KATHY YOUNG

PSYCHIC CATS?

On occasion cats have been observed becoming unusually agitated in the hours before an earthquake, scratching at doors or hurrying outside. The ancient Chinese used to rely on cats to predict natural disasters. It is not known exactly where these powers of prediction come from, but it is thought that cats may have a sensitivity to static electricity, magnetic fields or faint tremors which humans do not, and it is these that cause the cat's unusual behaviour.

CATS' INCREDIBLE JOURNEYS – 1

Like birds, and indeed many animals, cats often show a remarkable capacity to find their way home from many, many miles away. Scientific explanation of this uncanny ability varies; however, it is thought that it involves some combination of their innate biological clock, the angle of the sun, and sensing the earth's magnetic field. Some notable cat travellers include:

Sugar
Travelled 1,500 miles (2,400 kilometres) in fourteen months to be reunited with his owners who had moved to their new home in Oklahoma, USA.

Cookie
In six months, Cookie travelled 550 miles (885 kilometres) back to her home in Chicago, USA in 1949, after she was shipped to Wilber, Nebraska.

Howie
This plucky Persian traversed 1,000 miles (1,600 kilometres) of desert, rivers and wilderness in the Australian Outback to find his owner when she moved home.

Ling-Ling
This cat pursued his owner all the way from Sandusky, Ohio, USA, to the unknown territory of Orlando in Florida when he was left in the care of the owner's sister.

Buttons
In 1983, a black female cat called Buttons crawled under the bonnet of a neighbour's car and was not discovered until the driver stopped at a service station in Newcastle, Britain, six hours later. They were 280 miles (450 kilometres) from their home in Great Yarmouth. Luckily (and remarkably) the cat was unharmed and the driver continued his journey to Aberdeen with Buttons as a passenger. Upon their arrival, an airline that had heard their tale flew Buttons back to her owner free of charge.

Tom
Tenacious Tom traversed the United States, travelling approximately 2,500 miles (4,000 kilometres) from St Petersburg in Florida to find his owners in their new home in San Gabriel, California. It took him just over two years and his journey is thought to be the longest by a cat on record.

CATS' FOOD

If you put down food and the cat eats, it's hungry.
LARRY MADRID

∗ Because of the chlorine in tap water, it should be left to stand for twenty-four hours before being given to a cat – the chemical irritates parts of a cat's sensitive nose.

∗ Even though they can't taste them, cats love sweets.

∗ Cats are creatures of habit – they prefer to dine in the same place, at the same time, and in a quiet spot. A clean bowl is a must.

∗ Chocolate is toxic to a cat. As little as 16 ounces (450 grams) can kill a cat, and darker chocolate is more dangerous.

∗ Be wary of tinned cat food that is particularly red in colour. It may contain sodium nitrate, which is a carcinogen, and pet-food manufacturers are not required to list this chemical on their labels.

∗ Raw or undercooked meat and eggs are all as dangerous to cats as they are to humans.

∗ The average cat would, given the opportunity, consume about ten mice per day. This equates to approximately one cup of dry food or 10 ounces (280 grams) of canned food.

* Because cats
  require more
  protein than
  dogs, dog food
  should never be
  given to a cat.

* Cats cannot form
  Vitamin A from
  beta-carotene but,
  because a cat's diet
  must contain vitamins,
  a homemade diet must
  contains these essential
  elements, as a quality cat food
  from a reputable manufacturer will
  do. However, too many vitamins and minerals are just as
  dangerous as too few, so consult an animal nutritionist if
  unsure of the safe levels to administer.

* Water is a nutritional necessity – just a 15 per cent loss of
  water is enough to kill a cat.

* Smell is important in stimulating appetite. If a cat is ill, it
  may appear to go off food. This may occur because the
  inability to breathe or smell through a blocked nose may
  make the cat less inclined to eat. Similarly, canned food
  that has begun drying out and losing its smell may not be
  as appealing to a cat.

* Cats prefer sour, bitter, or salty tasting substances.

* Although a cat and a fish seems to be a traditional and
  customary pairing, in the desert, the wild cat's natural
  habitat, the cat would not have encountered fish; indeed,
  aside from a particular cat breed in India, wild cats will
  not hunt for fish even if they are available.

※ Unlike dogs or even humans, cats must eat meat to sustain their health, a consequence of its evolutionary development as a predator. Similarly, a steady supply of prey in the wild accounts for how a cat would traditionally dine on ten or more small meals a day. This reliance on a constant stream of food to provide all its dietary requirements has meant that there are certain substances cats can't produce in their own bodies, and which have to be supplied directly by its prey, including fat.

Famous Cat Owners – 1

Karel Čapek (1890–1938) The Czech dramatist, novelist and journalist Karel Čapek – the man who coined the word 'robot' – believed that cats had a magical hold over him. One day his Angora tomcat died as a result of eating poison, and later that day a female cat appeared at the writer's door. Čapek believed that there were two reasons for her fortuitous appearance in his life: to avenge the poisoned tomcat, and to replace that animal's life with her own. Čapek named the cat Pudlenka, and before long she had produced a total of twenty-six kittens; her daughter, Pudlenka II, had twenty-one.

Raymond Chandler (1888–1959) The American mystery writer referred to his black Persian cat, Taki, as his 'secretary', because she would sit on his manuscripts while he was trying to work on them. In the second of his detective novels, *Farewell, My Lovely* (1940), his hard-boiled yet honourable hero, Philip Marlowe, remarks of another character: 'He had a cat smile. But I like cats.'

Charles I (1600–49) This luckless King of England, Scotland and Ireland, whose obstinacy, double-dealing and lack of political nous plunged England into a long and bloody civil war (1642–6 and 1648–52), kept as a pet a black cat which he believed brought him luck – a somewhat superstitious belief for so deeply pious a man. Indeed, he was so afraid that the animal might run away or be stolen that he had it guarded day and night. On the day after the cat died, in November 1647, Charles was arrested on the orders of Parliament; on 30 January 1649 he was publicly beheaded on a scaffold erected in Whitehall, near the Houses of Parliament.

Sir Winston Churchill (1874–1965) Sir Winston owned a series of cats in his life, including one named Nelson who, during the Blitz (the intensive bombing of London and other British cities by the German Luftwaffe during the Second World War), showed little in common with the admiral after whom he was named, for he habitually hid under the bed during air raids. This led his master to comment, '[. . .]despite my most earnest and eloquent entreaties, I failed most utterly in persuading my friend before taking such craven action to give passing consideration to the name he bore.' In later life, Churchill owned a cat named Jock who attended many wartime Cabinet meetings. He referred to the cat as his special assistant and rumour has it that meals in the Churchill household could not begin until the ginger-coloured tabby was at the table. Jock was reported to have been lying on the bed at his master's side when, in January 1965, the great statesman died. Churchill left a clause in his will which stipulated that there should always be a marmalade cat in residence at Chartwell, his famous home in Kent. Churchill's other cats were named Blackie, Margate (see page 62) and Tango.

Colette (1873–1954) This was the pen name of the French writer Sidonie-Gabrielle Colette, whose most famous novel is probably *Gigi* (1944; English edition 1953), which was made into a successful musical and film. Colette adored cats, and often wrote about them in her books. She gave her own pets names like Fanchette, Zwerg, La Chatte (the French word for a female cat; it is also the title of a novel she published in 1933), and Chartreux, who was the last cat she owned. She told a friend after Zwerg died that 'We ought only to allow ourselves to become attached to parrots and tortoises', both animals that are famously long-lived; she also said that 'The only risk you ever run in befriending a cat is enriching yourself.' In *La Chatte* (published in English as *The Cat*, 1936), the main character, Alain, is forced to choose between Saha, a beautiful pure-bred Russian Blue, and his young bride, Camille. After Camille, furious with jealousy, tries to kill the cat, he chooses Saha.

Charles Dickens (1812–70) The great English novelist of the early to mid-Victorian era, Charles Dickens, owned a white cat which he initially christened William – that is, until 'he' had a litter of kittens, whereupon she was rechristened Williamina. Dickens was adamant that he would not keep any of the litter, but he was completely smitten by one female, which came to be known in the household as 'Master's Cat'. She would keep him company in his study while he wrote by candlelight, but would snuff out his candle with a deft paw when she wanted his attention.

Alexandre Dumas (1802–70) The author of *The Count of Monte Cristo*, *The Three Musketeers* and many other works, the French novelist and playwright Alexandre Dumas (known as 'Dumas *père*' to distinguish him from his son, also Alexandre and also a writer, and known, unsurprisingly, as 'Dumas *fils*') owned a cat called Mysouff. Mysouff possessed a considerable ability for telling the passage of time, and could predict when Dumas would finish work, even when his master was writing late at night.

[24]

T. S. Eliot (1888–1965) The British (though American born) poet, critic and playwright Thomas Stearns Eliot is perhaps best remembered for his long poems like *The Waste Land* and *The Love Song of J. Alfred Prufrock*. In 1939, however, he published a collection of poems for children about cats, under the title *Old Possum's Book of Practical Cats*. In 1981 this much loved book was set to music by Andrew Lloyd Webber (now Lord Lloyd-Webber) and, as the long-running and, for its time, record-breaking musical, *Cats*, won new audiences for the cat-loving Eliot's delightful poems. Eliot went on to be appointed to the Order of Merit and to be awarded the Nobel Prize in Literature; years after his death, royalties from *Cats* were to contribute significantly to his estate.

PURRING

Purring is commonly seen as a display of contentment on the part of a cat, but this may only be half the story. Scientists in America have discovered that the frequency at which cats purr helps their bones and organs to mend, creating a distinct evolutionary advantage. It also stimulates the skeletal system, which prevents the bones from weakening.

Cats' Ears

It can take up to two weeks after birth for the hearing of a newborn kitten to develop fully.

A human has six muscles to 'control' each ear – cats have thirty-two. Such control enables a cat to move and rotate its ears to pinpoint sound better. Each ear can rotate, independently of the other, a full 180 degrees, and at a rate many times faster than that of the most acute dog. It has been estimated that a cat's hearing capability is five times greater than that of a human.

The range of a cat's hearing stops at 65 kilohertz. Humans can only perceive sound that is less than 20 kilohertz in frequency.

Top Cats

If you are worthy of its affection, a cat will be your friend, but never your slave. – Théophile Gautier

As every cat owner knows, nobody owns a cat.
Ellen Perry Berkeley

The cat stands alone, distinct – out-individualizing every individual. – Elinor Mordaunt

Cats seem to go on the principle that it never does any harm to ask for what you want. – Joseph Wood Krutch

Last year a team of scientists published the results of an
extensive study of cat language. They determined that
although cats may demonstrate a wide variety of vocalizations,
they actually only have two phrases that are translatable
into human terms: 1. Hurry up with that food.
2. Everything here is mine.
ANONYMOUS

Cats never feel threatened. They are genetically incapable
of accepting that anyone could possibly dislike anything as
perfect as a cat. – KATHY YOUNG

People who belong to Siamese cats must make up their minds
to do a good deal of waiting upon them.
SIR COMPTON MACKENZIE

It is perhaps easier for a cat to train a man than for a man to
train a cat. A cat who desires to live with human beings makes
it his business to see that the so-called superior race behaves
in the proper manner toward him. – CARL VAN VECHTEN

Intelligence in the cat is underrated. – LOUIS WAIN

It's really the cat's house. I just pay the mortgage.
ANONYMOUS

Cat: a pygmy lion who loves mice, hates dogs and patronizes
human beings. – OLIVER HERFORD

There are many intelligent species in the universe.
They are all owned by cats. – ANONYMOUS

When I play with my cat, who knows whether she is not
amusing herself with me more than I with her?
MICHEL DE MONTAIGNE

You can keep a dog; but it is the cat who keeps people,
because cats find humans useful domestic animals.
GEORGE MIKES

As anyone who has ever been around a cat for any length of time
well knows, cats have enormous patience with the limitations of
the human kind. – CLEVELAND AMORY

Of all God's creatures there is only one that cannot be made the
slave of the lash. That one is the cat.
MARK TWAIN

Cats know how we feel; they just don't give a damn.
ANONYMOUS

CATS' CHAT

'My cat good' – this was a sentiment 'spoken' by Koko, a female
gorilla, who used sign language to tell her keepers about her
Manx kitten, which she named Lips-Lipstick.

There are many who believe that cats can 'talk', too. A famous
study by Mildred Moelk in 1944 made a number of curious
observations. She identified sixteen different and meaningful
sounds made by cats; a mixture of vowels, consonants and even
two dipthongs! There are many different variations of 'meow',
which most owners will recognize, and cats can change the
'meaning' of their 'meow' by altering the volume, tone, pitch,
rhythm and pronunciation.

Cats also have several other 'words' at their disposal beyond
'meow', including hissing, caterwauling, purring, growling and
mewing. A cat will also use a series of 'gestures' – posture, fur-
raising, facial expression – to modify or emphasize meaning. The
ability to communicate verbally may well have developed as a
result of feline domesticity, enabling the cat the better to cajole or
coerce its owner into fulfilling its needs and desires.

Moody Cats

Cats that have just been told off will often turn their backs on their owners and refuse to look at them. This 'mood' can also manifest itself in a refusal to come when called, and rigidity in the body when touched. However, the cat is not sulking. Rather, the posture and apparent 'attitude' is demonstrating that the owner dominates the cat, and that the cat accepts this situation. The refusal to face its owner stems not from 'wounded pride' but from fear; shouting at a cat is hostile behaviour and by turning its back the cat is attempting to avoid it.

Cat Naps

Cats are masterful sleepers, even from birth – new-born kittens sleep almost 90 per cent of the time. Even adult cats are asleep for approximately 60 per cent of their lives. Therefore, a fifteen-year-old cat has spent some nine years of its life sleeping!

While cats are sleeping they are still alert to external stimuli. If you disturb the tail of a sleeping cat it will respond accordingly.

During a period of deep sleep, a cat may twitch its whiskers, flex its paws or move its tail. Scientists who have studied the amount of electrical activity in the cat's brain during sleep have theorized that cats must dream.

More Cats

Cats are incredibly prolific – females become ill-tempered, nervous and may lose weight when not permitted to mate, while males become restless and dislike being kept indoors.

The solution to unwanted kittens is neutering and spaying – depending on the animal's sex, these procedures can be performed between six months to a year after the kitten has been born. This has the added advantage of extending a cat's lifespan by two or three years.

The maths says it all – a single female cat and her offspring, left undisturbed, would produce over 400,000 offspring in just seven years.

Cat pregnancy lasts for roughly nine weeks; that is, between sixty-two and sixty-five days from conception to birth.

A female feline is 'superfecund', which means she can mate with more than one male while in heat. This also means that a litter may consist of kittens who have different fathers.

The calico and tortoiseshell coats are sex-linked traits; the vast majority of cats displaying these coats are female, or else infertile males.

Cats Versus Dogs

Dogs come when they're called; cats take a message and get back to you later. – Mary Bly

A cat's sense of taste is keener than a dog's.

Cats are smarter than dogs. You can't get eight cats to pull a sled through snow. – Jeff Valdez

Scientific tests in the UK have concluded that while a dog's memory lasts only five minutes, a cat's recall can be as long as sixteen hours.

The difference between a cat and a dog. A dog thinks: 'They feed me, they shelter me, they love me, they must be gods.' A cat thinks: 'They feed me, they shelter me, they love me, *I* must be god.' – Anonymous

Cats are the ultimate narcissists. You can tell this because of all the time they spend on personal grooming. Dogs aren't like this. A dog's idea of personal grooming is to roll in a dead fish. James Gorman

Even the stupidest cat seems to know more than any dog. Eleanor Clark

When dogs leap on to your bed, it's because they adore being with you. When cats leap on to your bed, it's because they adore your bed. – Alisha Everett

While you might see a cat on a hot tin roof, a dog on a hot tin roof would be yowling its head off. Dr Bruce Fogle

A cat I find . . . is an easier companion than a dog. A cat's sense of independence also enables oneself to be independent. Derek Tangye

A cat will sit washing his face within two inches of a dog in the most frantic state of barking rage, if the dog be chained. Carl Van Vechten

The dog for the man, the cat for the woman.
ENGLISH PROVERB

By and large, people who enjoy teaching animals to roll over
will find themselves happier with a dog. – BARBARA HOLLAND

CATS AND MILK

Not all cats are milk lovers, despite the enduring perception of
'the cat and the cream'. Cow's milk is different from female cat's
milk, as in comparison cow's milk is deficient in protein.
Additionally, some cats are lactose intolerant, which for the
unlucky cat will result in diarrhoea.

A good way to avoid any problems is to feed a cat cream
instead, as it contains less lactose.

HAVING KITTENS

Leading up to the birth, the mother will try to find a suitable
nesting place; somewhere warm, dry and secluded.

Kittens emerge from their mother encased in a birth sac that the mother removes with her tongue.

The vigorous licking by the mother of her kittens warms and dries the small bodies and ensures that they do not catch a chill.

Don't be alarmed if the mother eats the placenta – a female wild cat would subsist on the nutrients contained in the placenta when kitten-rearing would prevent her from hunting.

The birth of a litter can take up to twenty-four hours.

Kittens are born with their eyes and ears sealed, but they should open within seven to ten days, and sometimes as quickly as two.

Newborn kittens rarely, if ever, foul the nest. This is because the young kittens have no control over their wastes, and urination and defecation only occur when the mother grooms under each kitten's tail, removing the waste in the process.

A kitten often seems to have a preference for a particular teat on its mother. This may simply be due to a pecking order among the litter in which the strongest kittens push their weaker siblings away from the most productive teats near the tail end of the mother's body.

It is not uncommon for related female cats to take care of each other's kittens, particularly when the litters are born at roughly the same time.

SOME CAT BEHAVIOURS

A cat's mood can be seen in its eyes. When frightened or excited, a cat will have large, round pupils. If you're feeling brave enough to look, an angry cat will have narrow pupils.

How a kitten is treated in its early years will affect its personality in the years to come.

A cat exposing its belly is a trusting cat.

Cats will lick themselves after being handled to get rid of the human scent.

Cat families usually play best in even numbers. Where possible, cats and kittens should be acquired in pairs.

Like humans, cats can get bored – they will show their boredom through excessive licking, chewing, or biting.

Cats will bury their faeces to cover their trail from predators.

Cats with long, lean bodies are more likely to be outgoing and more vocal than those with a stocky build.

Dead mice in the house? It is thought that most cats bring their prey into their owners' homes to protect it from other predators, and from an instinctive urge to return it to the nest for the young.

A cat will use scent glands near its 'cheeks' to mark people as well as furniture, so make the acquaintance of a cat (and garner its approval) when entering their territory.

Cats like being stroked because it reminds them of their mother's affection. Kittens are repeatedly licked by their mother during their earliest days and the action of human stroking causes the same sensation on their fur as feline licking.

The waving tail of a cat does not signify anger, but conflict. Two warring impulses – for example, the desire to roam outside, but the preference not to get wet in the rain – will cause the cat to stand still and wave its tail.

Cats' Curiosity

Does curiosity kill the cat? Well, one would hope not, but cats' natural curiosity can certainly get them into a lot of trouble. Whether being locked into suitcases and travelling on planes, or climbing on to precarious shelves and knocking over ornaments, cats certainly know how to get into mischief. Then there is their fascination with moving objects – unguarded fans and cats are a definite no-no.

However, according to tests performed by US veterinarian Donald Adams, the cat possesses a high level of intelligence and can remember problem solving-strategies to think its way around situations.

The cat has an excellent memory, and this particularly applies to inherited knowledge or something learned long ago but no longer used, such as how to hunt, or defend itself.

Some Cat Care

One litter tray per cat is the ideal ratio for a household with more than one cat.

Never pick a kitten up by the neck. Only a mother cat may do this safely. To pick up a cat or kitten correctly, place one hand behind its front legs, the other hand under its hindquarters, and lift gently.

Cats love to hear the sound of their own name and your voice, so talk to them.

To calm down a frightened cat, cover its eyes and forehead with your hand.

CATS' EYES

Most cats' eyes are greenish-yellow to gold. A deep green or brilliant copper colour is usually found only in pedigree cats who have been bred selectively, though it occurs occasionally in non-pedigree cats too.

To possess the eyes of a cat would mean wearing glasses for reading. Cats are long-sighted, and objects directly in front of them appear fuzzy and unclear. To compensate for this, their peripheral vision is extremely acute, and able to detect the slightest movement some distance away.

In relation to their bodies, cats have the largest eyes of any mammal.

The common belief that cats are colour-blind is false, as recent experiments have revealed that cats can see blue, green, and red.

Cats have a third eyelid called the nictitating membrane, though it is rarely visible. If it can be seen, it is sometimes an indication of ill health.

Cats cannot see directly under their noses, which is why they often cannot find food on the floor.

Contrary to popular belief, a cat cannot see in total darkness, but its vision in reduced light conditions is better than that of most animals. A cat can see some six times better at night than a

human, and needs only a sixth of the amount of light that a person does to make out the world around it.

All cats are born with blue eyes.

The reflective 'cats' eyes' that are placed on roads to aid driving at night are so called because a cat's eyes can appear to glow in the dark. This reflection occurs when even a small amount of light strikes the inner lining of the eye called the *tapetum lucidum*. This portion of the cat's eye maximizes the light available and is invaluable to a feline predator when hunting at night.

The eyes of a Siamese cat appear red in the dark. The reflective area in the retina lacks pigment, and the red colour is on account of the blood vessels present there.

As in the human eye, a cat's pupils contract and enlarge depending upon the amount of light, but whereas our eyes retain a circular shape, the cat's pupils narrow to vertical slits when in a bright environment.

How to Litter Train Your Cat

There are several simple things to do when training a kitten to use a litter tray. Firstly, after the kitten has eaten, immediately lift it up and gently place it inside the litter tray. This will reinforce the correct behaviour following a meal.

If an adult cat soils the floor next to the litter box, it may be because it doesn't feel comfortable using the tray. The tray must be clean and odour-free, and some cats prefer some litters to others. It may also help to have the tray in a quiet place. Clean a litter tray daily.

To Bath, or Not to Bath

Cats aren't clean, they are just covered in cat spit.
Anonymous

To bathe a cat takes brute force, perseverance, courage of conviction – and a cat. The last ingredient is usually hardest to come by. – Stephen Baker

Cat Fun

Cats do not need to be shown how to have a good time, for they are unfailingly ingenious in that respect.
James Mason

To demonstrate the truth of that quotation, here are just a few easily obtainable items that make excellent toys for cats.

* Paper (not plastic) bags without handles are great for pouncing on and hiding in.

* Catnip stuffed and sewn into an old sock will make most cats delirious with happiness.

* Plastic shower-curtain rings are fun either on their own, linked to others or tied to a piece of string and hung in an inviting spot.

* Reflected sunlight, such as from a watch or piece of jewellery, gives cats something to chase without you barely having to move! A torch beam is also great for this purpose.

* The tubes inside paper towels or toilet rolls will keep a cat happy, especially when it starts to shred.

* 'Fetch' isn't just a game for dogs; cats love it too. A ball of foil will make a satisfying noise, too.

* Any ball will satisfy a cat, although those with holes in will help the cat to carry the ball more easily. An empty bathtub provides a fascinating arena for a cat with its ball.

* Cats also love hide-and-seek. If there is more than one cat in the house, they will play this game for hours.

Hazardous Plants

While the cat is a creature well suited to the outdoors, sometimes their sheer enthusiasm and exuberance may lead them to sample plant life that they would do better to leave alone. Some may pose an obvious danger, but others, such as the tomato plant, may come as a surprise. One way of keeping your cat safe is to clear up any clippings or uprooted plants, as bulbs are often particularly hazardous. Even pollen can be dangerous: in England in 2005, a cat died after brushing against lilies in flower and getting pollen on its fur; when it licked itself clean it ingested the toxins in the pollen, which killed it.

Some Plants Poisonous to Cats – 1

Almond	Apricot	Belladonna	Bryony
Amaryllis	(stone)	Bird of	Buckthorn
Anemone	Asian Lily	Paradise	Buttercup
Angels'	Avocado	Black-eyed	
Trumpets	Azalea	Susan	
Angel Wings	Baneberry	Bloodroot	
Apple (seed)	Beech	Box	

Cat and Mouse

A mouse in the paws is worth two in the pantry. – Louis Wain

Okay, cats will never bring you pictures they've drawn in school, but they may give you a dead mouse. What parent could resist that gift? – Terri L. Haney

People who hate cats will come back as mice in their next life.
Faith Resnick

The clever cat eats cheese and breathes down rat-holes with baited breath. – W. C. Fields

Famous Cat Owners – 2

Ernest Hemingway (1899–1961) The American novelist and short-story writer Ernest Hemingway was noted for the harsh and unsentimental style of his writing, yet he had a decidedly soft streak when it came to cats. He owned thirty, one of them a polydactyl (see page 59) female he christened Princess Six Toes, and which he had been given by a ship's captain. Hemingway's home on Key West, one of the islands off the southern tip of Florida, USA is now a museum dedicated to the writer's life and work. There are presently some sixty cats living there, many of them descended from Hemingway's six-toed pet cat, and of these around half are polydactyl.

Victor Hugo (1802–85) One of the giants of French literature, the novelist, poet and dramatist Victor Hugo, author of such works as *Les Miserables* and *Notre-Dame de Paris*, is regarded as a national institution in the country of his birth. Like so many writers, he too loved cats, and wrote affectionately about his own in his diaries.

Samuel Johnson (1709–84) The great English man of letters Doctor Samuel Johnson was blessed with a generous spirit and a kind heart, although he rarely tolerated fools. From an unpromising start in penury he rose to become the pre-eminent figure in the literary life of eighteenth-century England, with works that encompassed journalism, poetry, essays, criticism, satire, and even a novel; he was also, famously, the compiler of the world's first practical dictionary. Johnson was devoted to his pet cat, Hodge, to whom he liked to feed oysters and other treats.

Edward Lear (1812–88) Although Edward Lear was a prominent painter of landscapes and of birds and animals, he is best remembered for his writings for children, and especially his light verse, and as the popularizer of the limerick. His *A Book of Nonsense* was published in 1845, followed by *Nonsense Songs, Stories, Botany and Alphabets* in 1871 – in which his most famous poem, 'The Owl and the Pussycat', first appeared; *More Nonsense, Pictures, Rhymes, Botany etc.* later the same year, and *Laughable Lyrics* in 1877; he also wrote travel books which, like his poems, he illustrated himself. A somewhat melancholy man prone to loneliness, Lear was devoted to his tabby cat, Foss, who became a part of his master's solitary life, and who was the inspiration for the cat in 'The Owl and the Pussycat'; Lear's drawings of Foss accompany the poem. As cats go, Foss was no beauty; according to Lear, he wore an almost constantly startled expression, was somewhat corpulent, and had a shortened tail, thanks to a superstitious servant who believed that this mutilation would stop poor Foss from straying. Foss shared seventeen years of his master's wanderings – it was said that he would roll on the pages of Lear's manuscripts to dry the ink with his fur – and in return Lear's devotion to his feline companion was so great that when he decided to move to San Remo in Italy, where he built a house in which he spent the last seven years of his life, he gave instructions that the new building should be laid out like his old home in England, so that Foss would not suffer any confusion or uncertainty in unfamiliar surroundings. When Foss died in 1887 he was buried with due ceremony in his master's Italian garden. Lear did not long outlive his beloved pet, dying some two months later.

Sir Isaac Newton (1692–1727) The great English 'natural philosopher' (i.e. scientist) and mathematician, Sir Isaac Newton, still revered for his laws of motion and gravity, for his studies of light and for his work on what became the basis for calculus, loved cats and cared greatly for their welfare. In order that he should not be interrupted in his work by having to open the door to an importunate pet, he invented the cat flap (or cat door), thereby allowing his cats to come and go freely through closed doors. He also made a smaller cat flap for kittens to use after his cats produced litters.

Marilyn Monroe (1926–62) Having made her name in Hollywood, the American model, actress and, now, icon, lived for a time in New York in the 1950s, where she kept a Persian cat named Mitsou. Her fame, however, sometimes gave her problems if she had to call a vet to tend to the animal, as she noted: 'They think I'm kidding when I say "This is Marilyn Monroe. My cat's having kittens." They think I'm some kind of nut and hang up.'

Florence Nightingale (1820–1910) The English nurse and hospital reformer Florence Nightingale, known as 'the Lady of the Lamp' after the part she played in nursing sick and wounded British troops during the Crimean War of 1853–6, owned more than sixty cats during her long lifetime. She named all of them after famous people of her day, so that her pets included 'Disraeli' and 'Gladstone' (respectively British Prime Ministers 1868 and 1874–80, and 1868–74, 1880–5, 1886, and 1892–4), as well as a large Persian cat named 'Bismarck', after Prince Otto von Bismarck, the 'Iron Chancellor' of the new German Empire from 1871 until 1890.

Some Male Cat Names

Ali	Duke	Kit	Sam
Alfie	Eliot	Leo	Smudge
Angus	Elvis	Louis	Sooty
Archie	Ernie	Magic	Spotty
Barney	Evil	Max	Tigger
Basil	Fatty	Mouser	Tom Cat
Bertie	Felix	Nicky	Top Cat
Billy	Frankie	Percy	Wesley
Boss	Fred	Poirot	Whiskers
Browne	Herman	Rascal	Whiskey
Buster	Jack	Reggie	
Charlie	Jake	Rocky	

Catty!

Do our cats name us? My former husband swore that Humphrey and Dolly and Bean Blossom called me The Big Hamburger.
Eleanora Walker

Cats always know whether people like or dislike them. They do not always care enough to do anything about it.
Winifred Carrière

Cats are just little hair factories.
Jim Davis

Not for the Squeamish

* Fleas were probably responsible for the bubonic plague, and, as such, should not be welcome on your cat!

* Under optimum conditions, flea eggs may survive for more than ten years.

* Carpets are the ideal environment for eggs and pupae to survive for long periods of time.

* Two out of three fleas are female.

* A female flea can consume fifteen times her body weight in blood daily.

GETTING RID OF FLEAS

It's easy to mistake flea bites for a rash; both have a small red spot in the middle, surrounded by a red area. If such bites appear on you or on a family member, then it is possible that your cat has fleas. Cats can be infected by other cats, or simply by passing through an area in which other infected animals have travelled. Only animals with an allergy to flea bites will scratch when they have fleas, so even though your cat may not to be in discomfort, it may still be infested. Furthermore, irritation is not just an aggravation for your animal, as extreme sensitivity may lead to weight loss and intense discomfort.

Flea larvae can live off various organic matter, including dried blood and hair and skin cells. After a number of developmental stages, the larvae pupate by spinning a cocoon from which an adult flea emerges. Effective flea control involves considering two factors – the cat and the house.

There are several options for treating a cat. The first one involves a regular treatment with a cat-specific insecticide, usually to the neck. One insecticide introduces a hormone into the cat's bloodstream that prevents the eggs from hatching. Other treatments, usually administered to a spot between the cat's shoulder blades, secrete chemicals along with a cat's natural bodily oils, and these chemicals kill fleas on contact. Cat shampoos, powders and sprays are also effective – however, flea collars are now widely considered to be useless. Simple combing and bathing of the cat will also remove many of the parasites.

Look after your living environment by washing all cat bedding thoroughly, including any mattress or cushions your cat may have. Vacuuming daily is vital, and in particularly bad cases of infestation, a thorough steam clean may be necessary – but remember to treat the whole house, not just the 'cat' areas.

CATNIP

Catnip (*Nepeta cataria*; also known as catmint) is a perennial herb, a member of the mint family native to temperate areas of the world. Not all catnip is the same. There are in fact many types of catnip, each with a different taste. In the seventeenth and eighteenth centuries catnip tea was thought to have medicinal powers, and it was often prescribed for a wide range of human ailments.

The active ingredient in catnip is nepetalactone, which is a terpene, naturally occurring compounds in plants associated with fragrances and found in essential oils; it is non-toxic and non-addictive. Not all cats react to it; those that do appear to enter a trancelike state. However, the usual reaction involves the cat licking, biting and chewing the catnip, rubbing against it and rolling on it repeatedly, purring, meowing and even leaping in the air.

A cat's response is believed to come about because proximity to the plant or its leaves – even dried leaves – stimulates a female sex pheromone; interestingly, the big cats seem to have the same reaction as domestic cats.

The effects can last for about six minutes, although the animal's response is at its most intense for the first few minutes. Cats of reproductive age are more sensitive to catnip than cats that are very young or very old. Generally, males demonstrate a greater reaction to contact with the plant than females, while kittens under six months old show no interest in it at all.

Not every cat gets a high from catnip. Felines that lack a specific dominant gene – approximately 20 per cent of domestic cats – will demonstrate no reaction to catnip at all.

The best way to provide your cats with catnip is to buy fresh cuttings of the plant. If you are using fresh catnip, squeeze it between your fingers in order to release the oils in the herb, and place a small piece on the floor.

You can buy cat toys filled with catnip; however, these are not particularly effective and the dried herb inside tends to go stale. Alternatively, a spray form of catnip can be applied to scratching posts or toys to stimulate play and get your cat interested in such activities. You can, of course, also buy seeds and grow your own catnip, either in pots or in the garden

PHOTOGRAPHING YOUR CAT

You will need either to get down to the same level as your cat, or to place him (or her, of course) on a tallish piece of furniture such as a high table or chest of drawers, so that camera lens and pet are at the same level. This takes patience; independent-minded animals that they are, cats will not necessarily stay in place, or stay still, simply because you want to photograph them.

Avoid direct eye contact and don't make any sudden or aggressive moves, especially if your cat is at all shy or timid.

Try throwing him a catnip-stuffed toy and press the shutter

while he is in mid-air. Cats in action make for some of the best photos, although most first efforts will capture only part of your cat, until you get the hang of action photography.

For a more dignified photo – and all cats excel at looking regal – place the animal on a cushion and get down to his level. Always move in close – your cat should take up at least half of the frame – and ensure that there is plenty of light directed at the cat's face; however, this does not meaning shining a strong light in his face, as he will naturally turn away from, say, a powerful lamp shining in his eyes.

A neutral background is best for photographing a black cat, as a dark background will make the entire photo too dark, while a white background will provide too much contrast, which will emphasize the blackness and lack of detail. Also, if you are using a flash don't snap a black cat against a wall – if the animal is too close, the shadow on the wall behind him will blend into his body.

CATTY PROBLEMS SOLVED

A water pistol can be useful if you catch your cat in the act of clawing the furniture. Don't let your pet see you using the pistol, though, as this may cause the animal stress, or will otherwise simply teach it to scratch when you are not around.

A cat that paws or digs at the carpet by a closed door may be asking to be let out. It is best not to take this hint – if you do, the cat will come to think that its behaviour is acceptable, and will go on doing it.

A cat can do considerable damage to wooden furniture if it decides to use some part as a favourite scratching post. Try treating the affected area with vinegar or other strong-smelling liquids; a pad soaked in eucalyptus oil, or even half an orange, at the site of the damage can be effective. (Make sure first, though, by testing it on a hidden part, that the liquid you use won't damage the affected piece of furniture).

Upholstered or fabric-covered furniture will suffer even more if used by your cat as a scratching post. Some people recommend covering the scratching area with aluminium kitchen foil, or even

with a different fabric; otherwise, using double-sided tape at the site may work, since a cat doesn't like the unpleasant feeling of stickiness on its pads.

Prevention is better than counter-measures, however. The moment you see your cat beginning to scratch where it shouldn't, gently but firmly redirect it to an alternative of your own choosing, such as a scratching post, board, or mat. The cat will very quickly learn to associate its scratching activities with the area you have selected.

A different technique is required if your cat is scratching to gain attention, as some do. It is natural when this happens to shout at the animal to make it stop; however, it is much better to ignore him, or even to leave the room, which will quickly teach him that such attention-seeking ploys won't work.

You often hear people say that they are allergic to cats, and certainly being in a cat's, or cats', presence can produce typical allergic reactions in such people. In actual fact, what they are allergic to is not the animals themselves, but to cat saliva or to the dead skin flakes, known as 'dander', in cats' fur. Any allergic reaction will be reduced if the cat is bathed regularly, using a good-quality cat shampoo.

CATS VERSUS HUMANS

An ordinary kitten will ask more questions than any
five-year-old boy. – CARL VAN VECHTEN

A cat has absolute emotional honesty: human beings,
for one reason or another may hide their feelings,
but a cat does not.
ERNEST HEMINGWAY

A cat's heart beats almost twice as fast as a human heart –
about 140 to 240 times a minute in the average cat.

If man could be crossed with a cat it would improve man,
but it would deteriorate the cat. – MARK TWAIN

Cats are kindly masters, just so long as you remember
your place. – PAUL GRAY

I've never understood why women love cats. Cats are
independent, they don't listen, they don't come in when you call,
they like to stay out all night, and when they're home they like
to be left alone and sleep. In other words, every quality that
women hate in a man, they love in a cat. – JAY LENO

The playful kitten, with its pretty little tigerish gambols, is infinitely more amusing than half the people one is obliged to live with in the world. – LADY SYDNEY MORGAN

A cat knows you are the key to his happiness . . .
a man thinks he is. – ANONYMOUS

A cat has 250 bones in its body, compared to 206 in humans, which is why they can bend and twist more than humans.

If human, cats might play solitaire, but they would never sit around with the gang and a few six-packs watching *Monday Night Football*. – *Time* magazine, 7 December, 1981

I have studied many philosophers and many cats.
The wisdom of cats is infinitely superior. – HIPPOLYTE TAINE

Cats are much more at home in a warmer climate. They can tolerate a skin temperature of 126° Fahrenheit (52° Celsius) before they start to feel uncomfortable; anything over 113° Fahrenheit (45° Celsius) is too hot for most humans.

Thousands of years ago, cats were worshipped as gods.
Cats have never forgotten this. – ANONYMOUS

I love cats. I even think we have one at home.
EDWARD L. BURLINGAME

In a cat's eye, all things belong to cats. – ENGLISH PROVERB

SOME FAMOUS CATS

Atossa
The English poet Matthew Arnold (1822–88) immortalized his Persian cat, Atossa, in his 1882 poem 'Poor Matthias', about the death of his canary. In the poem, Arnold recalls how his old cat would sit motionless for hours beside the canary's cage, never attempting to attack it, but never abandoning the hope that one day the bird would fall into his clutches.

Brownie
When its owner died in 1963, Brownie, of San Diego, California, became one of the richest cats in the world, inheriting US $415,000 (£217,000 at today's rates) under the terms of the will.

Cato
According to at least two websites, this Californian Spangled cat was bought for the record sum of US $24,000 (£12,500 today;

about £15,000 then) in January 1987, and eleven years later, in February 1998, became the new record holder as the world's most expensive cat.

Selima
Selima was a cat owned by the English writer Horace Walpole. With his friend, the poet Thomas Gray (1716–71), famous for his long poem *Elegy Written in a Country Churchyard*, Walpole made the Grand Tour of Europe in 1747, during which his beloved cat drowned in a goldfish bowl. To commemorate this sad event, Gray wrote a poem, 'Ode on the Death of a Favourite Cat Drowned in a Tub of Gold Fishes', which gave to the language the (slightly misquoted) expression, 'All that glitters is not gold.' Confusingly, the poet describes Selima both as a tortoiseshell and a tabby.

Timothy
A white cat that was a favourite pet of the British detective-story writer Dorothy L. Sayers (1893–1957). He features in two of her poems, 'For Timothy' and 'War Cat'.

Trim
This cat was born aboard the Royal Navy ship HMS *Reliance* in 1799 near the Cape of Good Hope and was adopted by Matthew Flinders (1774–1814), the ship's assistant surgeon. Flinders would go on to become one of the leading explorers and surveyors of his age.

Trim accompanied his master in his circumnavigation of Australia, and, when Flinders was detained, after a shipwreck, by the French in Mauritius, shared his captivity. The explorer described his much-loved cat as 'one of the finest animals I ever saw . . . [his] robe was a clear jet black, with the exception of his four feet, which seemed to have been dipped in snow, and his under lip, which rivalled them in whiteness. He had also a white star on his breast.' In 1995 a statue of Trim was erected in Sydney, paid for by public subscription.

Trixie

A black-and-white cat belonging to the English soldier Henry Wriothesley, third Earl of Southampton (1573–1624), during the reigns of Elizabeth I and James VI and I. When the Earl was imprisoned, under sentence of death, in the Tower of London for treason, Trixie, faithful to her master, decided to keep him company. It is said that during the two years of his incarceration she made her way across London and descended to his cell via the chimney, though Southampton's wife may have helped her with her travels. The Earl was so impressed with the cat's loyalty that before his release he commissioned a portrait of himself and his beloved pet together in his cell.

CATS' LEGS AND PAWS

While a cat's legs are short compared to the length of its body, they are powerful. Strong muscles can produce explosive power for leaping on prey or for great bursts of speed, and this is augmented by the sharp angles of the knee and heel of the hind legs.

Cat forelegs can be stretched wide apart to hug the body of a kill and hold it close, and the paws are suited for great flexibility too. Most cats have five 'toes' in the forepaws and four in the hind paws; however, some domestic cats, especially in the north-eastern United States, have extra toes inside their front feet, and

sometimes even on their hind feet. This inherited mutation is known as 'polydactylism' and is often prized by owners.

The prevalence of polydactyl cats on America's East Coast is believed to have come about because of sailors' preference for such cats as mousers aboard merchant vessels. These cats have since continued to breed more numerously in sea ports.

Cats in High Office

Tabby

When Abraham Lincoln, sixteenth President of the United States of America (1809–65), assumed presidential office in 1861 he was accompanied by his son's cat, Tabby, the first of four cats Lincoln was to have at the White House.

Home Office Fat Cat

Since the late 1920s, the British Civil Service has kept a series of official documents detailing the upkeep of its cats employed on government service. On 3 June 1929, a request was made for an allowance of one penny (1d, less than 0.5p) per day for a mouser named Peter, based at the Home Office. He was then succeeded by a series of male cats with the same name, until, in 1964, a pedigree Manx female was appointed and given the name Peta. Her 'aristocratic' temperament as 'a member of a non-industrial grade', however, led her to neglect her duties; as a result, in February 1967 an official memorandum was sent out ordering staff not to feed her titbits as she had become 'inordinately fat'. None the less, a certain sentimentality, if not affection, must have penetrated the mandarin mind, for Peta kept her job until 1976, when she was retired to the country.

Humphrey

Few cats have the chance to make the national news, but when Humphrey, the official mouser to the Cabinet Office and long-time resident of No. 10 Downing Street, the Prime Minister's official London home, disappeared, he did just that.

A long-haired black-and-white cat, Humphrey arrived at No. 10 as a stray when Margaret Thatcher was still Prime Minister, and stayed – apart from the odd disappearance – throughout the term of her successor, John Major. He also spent several months of 1997 in the household of Major's successor as Prime Minister, Tony Blair, following Labour's victory over the Conservatives in the General Election of May that year. Rumours that the latter's wife, Cherie, was allergic to cats were denied by the Prime Minister's office. In November, however, Humphrey retired, apparently for health reasons, and went to live in the home of a civil servant in South London. Needless to say the Conservative Party, which was by now the Opposition to Blair's Labour government, made much of this, claiming that Humphrey had 'voted with his paws', and that after eight contented years under a Tory administration he had only been able to take six months of Labour rule 'before he lost interest in living'.

Humphrey's disappearance that brought him fame and the attention of the media had happened some two years earlier, in 1995. On that occasion he was eventually found, after being missing for three months, at the Royal Army Medical College, then the headquarters of the Royal Army Medical Corps, on Millbank, not far from the Houses of Parliament. Recognized, probably as a result of all the press attention, he was taken back to No. 10 Downing Street. By then, however, he was probably the most famous cat in the land, and one whom the British public had taken to their hearts.

India

India belongs to the family of President George W. Bush, and lives in the White House in Washington, DC, the official residence of US Presidents. Ernie, a young polydactyl cat (polydactyly is the condition, in people or animals, of having an extra digit on each hand, foot or paw), is also a pet of the family. Ernie's somewhat unrestrained behaviour, however, especially his furniture-scratching, was thought to be a little extreme for the august dignity of the White House, with the result that he was sent to live with a friend of the Bushes in Century City, California.

Margate

When a stray black kitten appeared on the doorstep of No. 10 Downing Street in 1953, the Prime Minister, Sir Winston Churchill, seeing it as a sign of good luck, immediately adopted him. Since he had just returned from delivering an important speech at Margate in Kent, Churchill named the kitten in the town's honour. Within ten days, Margate had managed to advance himself to a favoured position on his new master's bed.

Shan

A Siamese, Shan was the pet of Susan, daughter of Gerald Ford, President of the United States from 1974 to 1976.

Siam

The first Siamese cat to appear in the United States was the gift of the American Consul in Bangkok, the capital of what was then Siam (now Thailand), to the nineteenth President of the United States, Rutherford B. Hayes (1822–93).

Slippers

Slippers, the much-loved pet of US President Theodore Roosevelt (1858–1919), was, like President George W. Bush's Ernie, another polydactyl cat, having an extra toe on each paw. Self-confident to the point of arrogance, one evening he forced an entire procession of important White House guests to make a detour around his recumbent form.

Socks

Another White House cat, Socks, a black-and-white animal of no determinate breed, was the pet of Chelsea Clinton, daughter of US President William Jefferson (Bill) Clinton (b. 1946; President 1993–2001) and his wife Hillary (herself now a US Senator). Joining the household in 1993, Socks was the first cat to live at the White House since Misty Malarky Ying Yang, the improbably named pet of Amy Carter, wife of President Jimmy Carter, who left presidential office in 1981. Socks became a favourite of the American public, enjoying his own fan club, serving as the guide to the 'White House for Kids' website and, it was said, receiving 75,000 letters and parcels each week. In 1993 a light-hearted book by Michael O'Donoghue and J. C. Suares purporting to be the First Cat's own journal, *Socks Goes to Washington: The Diary of America's First Cat*, was published in the USA.

In 1996 President Clinton won a second term in office, which brought about a major change in Socks's status with the arrival of a new family pet, Buddy, a chocolate-coloured Labrador. Worse was to come, for when Clinton's term as President ended in 2001, Buddy stayed on as a member of the Clinton family, but for Socks the writing was on the wall. Chelsea was not permitted to take her cat with her to Stanford University, and it was said that the cat and the upstart Labrador were rather less than good friends. One of them had to go and, sadly for Socks, it was him. Luckily, he was found a home with Betty Currie, Clinton's White House Secretary, who took him to live with her in the Washington suburb of Virginia.

Tom Kitten

Tom Kitten was the pet of Caroline Kennedy, the daughter of US President John F. Kennedy (1917–63). On his death in 1962, Tom Kitten received an obituary in the press. His master did not long outlive him, falling to an assassin's bullet in Dallas, Texas, in November 1963.

SOME PLANTS POISONOUS TO CATS – 2

Cactus	Chrysanthemum	Croton
Caladium	Clematis	Crocus
Castor plant	Colchicum	Cup of Gold
Cestrum	Columbine	Cycads
Cherry (stone,	Conium	Cyclamen
seed and leaf)	Corncockle	Daffodil
Chinaberry	Cornflower	Daphne

CELEBRITY CATS

Morris the Cat

Morris the Cat, a large orange-striped tabby, is one of the most famous cats in advertising, being the mascot of 9Lives cat food, an American product. With his cultured voice and pampered-pet attitude, he has been a favourite with the US public since he first hit TV screens in 1969, while his importance to his company is shown by the fact that his name is a registered trademark (as is 9Lives), and appears in advertising and promotions as 'Morris® the Cat'.

Actually, the original Morris has been dead since 1975. He had been 'discovered' in 1968 at an animal shelter in Lombard, Illinois, where officials thought he had such star quality that that they contacted a professional animal handler, Bob Martwick, who worked for the Leo Burnett Advertising Agency. Martwick thought so too, and rescued Lucky – as the cat was then called – from a dull and probably short life at the shelter, and began grooming him for the 9Lives cat-food account.

9Lives was equally taken with Morris, and in particular with the campaign that the agency had created, one of the most successful TV-advertising campaigns in history. To cap it all, the American public fell in love with the fastidious character personified by Morris, with the result that he became the best

known and most recognizable cat in the USA. There have been several Morrises since the death of the original in 1975 (his immediate successor was Harry the Cat), and the current one lives in California with his handler and trainer.

Morris's career was not confined to TV commercials alone, for he also appeared in the 1972 movie *Shamus* with Burt Reynolds and Dyan Cannon, while a life of him, *Morris: An Intimate Biography* by Mary Daniels, was published in 1974; later, in the 1980s, he appeared as the author of a number of books about cat care and health. As time passed he became a favourite with the media – *Time* Magazine called him 'the feline Burt Reynolds', although it is not known how the finicky Morris might have taken that – appearing in numerous magazines as well as on the cover of *Cat Fancy*'s thirtieth-anniversary issue. In 1991 he even hosted a primetime television special, and he has been awarded a PATSY, the American Humane Society's Picture Animal Top Star Award. He also allegedly campaigned for the Presidency of the United States in 1988 and again in 1992.

Orangey
By all accounts intolerant and demanding, Orangey achieved his greatest fame as 'Cat', the pet of Holly Golightly, the scatty call girl

played by Audrey Hepburn in the film *Breakfast at Tiffany's* (1961). For all the charm of his screen performance, Orangey was apparently so bad-tempered and difficult to work with that even his owner, Frank Inn, disliked him. Nevertheless, because he had won two PATSYs (see Morris the Cat, above), he gained a reputation as one of the best animal actors in the world.

Syn

Syn, a Siamese, earned a PATSY (see Morris the Cat, above) for playing the title role of 'DC' in the 1965 Walt Disney film *That Darn Cat!*, which starred Hayley Mills and Dean Jones. A 1997 remake (without the exclamation mark in the title) starred Christina Ricci and Doug E. Doug, and was generally panned.

CAT LEGENDS

Ra, both the supreme deity and the sun god of the ancient Egyptians, was believed to battle each night with the Serpent of Darkness, for which he would adopt the form of a tomcat.

According to one legend, the Prophet Muhammad was saved from the bite of a deadly snake by a cat. On another occasion, the Prophet cut off the sleeve of his robe in order not to awaken a sleeping kitten when he stood up.

In another legend, Muhammad rested his hand lightly on the brow of his favourite breed of cat, a tabby. As a result, so the legend runs, tabbies have borne an 'M' mark on their foreheads ever since.

A Christian legend, however, suggests that it was the Virgin Mary who, as a reward to the cat that purred the infant Jesus to sleep, ordained that from that time on all tabbies should wear a letter 'M' on their foreheads.

The Cat is one of the signs in the twelve-year cycle of animals that makes up the Vietnamese zodiac. The most recent Year of the Cat fell between 16 February 1999 and 4 February 2000, and those born under the sign are said to be blessed with patience and a quick and flexible mind.

There is no Cat in the Chinese zodiac, however. As the Chinese legend goes, the Rat had the task of inviting the animals to the Jade Emperor's palace, where it was to be decided which of them would be chosen for the zodiac. Unfortunately, the Rat forgot to invite the Cat, with the result that the Cat has been the Rat's sworn enemy ever since.

The persecution of witches in seventeenth-century France brought in its wake the persecution of their supposed 'familiars', cats, especially black ones. Although Cardinal Richelieu (1585–1642), Minister of State to Louis XIII, was one of the most powerful men in the country, he harboured a great fondness for cats (see also page 88). It is this, perhaps, that led to the legend that the Cardinal's black cat, Lucifer, used to smuggle cats on to ships bound for North America.

A similar legend tells of a cat named Aristofanus (also known as Mange), who is alleged to have saved 2,000 cats from persecution at the time of the witchcraft trials by hiding them in an abandoned barn. It is also said that on the hideout's discovery, Aristofanus and his fellows fled to the forest, where they established a cat colony that has remained untouched ever since.

It's a Cat's World – 2

Cat lovers can readily be identified. Their clothes always look old and well used. Their sheets look like bath towels, and their bath towels look like a collection of knitting mistakes.
Eric Gurney

Few animals display their mood via facial expressions as distinctly as the cat. – Konrad Lorenz

I gave my cat a bath the other day. He sat there, he enjoyed it, it was fun for me. The fur would stick to my tongue, but other than that . . . – STEVE MARTIN

We have two cats. They're my wife's cats, Mischa and Alex. You can tell a woman names a cat like this. Women always have sensitive names: Muffy, Fluffy, Buffy. Guys name cats things like Tuna Breath, Fur Face, Meow Head. They're nice cats. They've been neutered and they've been declawed. So they're like pillows that eat. – LARRY REEB

Men and dogs will never understand what a woman sees in a cat.
ANONYMOUS

If toast always lands butter-side down, and cats always land on their feet, what happen if you strap toast on the back of a cat and drop it? – STEVEN WRIGHT

Cats do not think that they are little people. They think that we are big cats. This influences their behaviour in many ways.
ANONYMOUS

The only self-cleaning thing in this kitchen is the cat.
ANONYMOUS

CATS' SKIN AND FUR

* Cats can have freckles. They can appear anywhere on a cat's skin, even in the mouth.

* The Persian cat has the longest and thickest fur of all domestic cats. The top coat may grow up to 5 inches (13 centimetres) long.

* Cats' fur consists of two layers, an undercoat and a top coat.

* Cats can get 'age spots', like humans. These manifest as black spots on the skin that appear around the lips, eyes, and nose, and usually occur when the cat is between three to five years of age.

CAT MYTHS

Myth: A cat uses its whiskers in order to maintain its balance.

Fact: A cat uses its whiskers to 'feel' its way – for instance, when judging the width of a gap it wants to go through – but they have no effect on its balance, one way or the other.

Myth: A cat will always land on its feet.

Fact: It is true that a falling cat will instinctively twist in the air so that it lands feet first. Many will survive falls from high places, but equally, cats are often hurt or even killed as the result of such falls. Anyone who lives above first-storey level and who keeps cats should think of using some kind of screening on balconies and windows.

Myth: Pregnant women should not own a cat.

Fact: Some cats are infected with a disease called toxoplasmosis, which is caused by a parasite called *Toxoplasma gondii*. Toxoplasmosis can be harmful to unborn infants whose mothers are infected with the parasite just before or during pregnancy, although if it is caught before or after this time it is usually harmless to both mother and infant. As long as a pregnant woman handles the litter tray with care, or, better still, avoids it altogether, there is no reason why she shouldn't own a cat.

Myth: A spayed or neutered cat will invariably gain weight.

Fact: Like most animals, including humans, cats get fat either by eating too much, or by not exercising enough, or by a combination of both. These sterilizing operations are often performed on cats at an age when their metabolic rates have slowed down, meaning they need less food than younger animals. As a result, if the cat continues to eat the amount of food it has been used to before the operation, it may gain weight. You can help a spayed or neutered cat to stay fit by making sure that it doesn't overeat and that it gets plenty of exercise.

Myth: Cats cannot get rabies.

Fact: This is untrue. Most warm-blooded mammals, including cats, can carry rabies. Cats, like dogs, should be vaccinated against rabies.

Myth: Cats heal themselves by licking their wounds.

Fact: The antibacterial properties of saliva will prevent or help to prevent abscess formation in wounds, so in this respect licking will go some way to helping a wound to heal. However, after three or four days of such licking, the cat should be discouraged from continuing this activity to enable new skin to grow. A bitter-tasting product should be applied to the skin around the wound.

Some Cat Luck and Lore

* In Transylvania, Romania, it is said that if a cat jumps over a corpse, the dead person will rise again as a vampire.

* You will always be lucky if you can make friends with cats.

* In the Middle Ages, some Europeans believed that cats had healing powers. Those people with a diagnosis of 'insanity' were sometimes given cats to own as a means of treatment.

* If a cat voluntarily comes to your house, ensure that you welcome it in – sending the cat away will bring you bad luck.

* Early Christianity taught that a cat seen on a grave meant that the buried person's soul was under the Devil's control.

* If two cats were seen fighting around a dying person, or near a grave shortly after a funeral, this represented the Devil and an angel fighting for possession of the recently departed soul.

* A new cat given the name of a recently deceased cat will bring you good luck.

* Cat lore in ancient Thailand taught that when a particularly spiritual or holy person died, their soul would enter the body of a cat, and would then ascend to Paradise when the cat died.

* If you kick a cat you will develop an illness in the leg used to strike out.

* The ancient Egyptians believed that cats captured the light of the setting sun in their eyes, and preserved it until morning.

* To have a cat follow you home is good luck.

* Legend has it that the Manx breed lost its tail as a result of boarding Noah's Ark, when the door closed on its tail.

SOME MORE CAT HISTORY

It is believed that some cat behaviours and traits, including their love of warmth and of sunning themselves, and disposing of their faeces in sandy places, all stem from when their ancestor, the wild cat, lived in desert climates.

The first associations of cats with humans may have begun toward the end of the Stone Age. It took many centuries, however, for the cat to become established as a domestic animal.

Phoenician cargo ships are thought to have brought the first domesticated cats to Europe around 900 BC when their coastal trade routes included Gaul (France), and Kernow (Cornwall), from where the traders acquired tin for the manufacture of weaponry. While they were items of trade, the cats also suppressed pest numbers on board ships.

Phoenician traders first acquired cats during a revolt in 1100 BC which resulted in Phoenician independence from Egypt. Smuggling abroad the cats they had seized must have been dangerous, because the Egyptian penalty for exporting cats was death.

The Egyptians were so protective of their sacred cats that they would send soldiers to recover those that had been snatched by the traders. Consequently, the Phoenicians needed to set up breeding catteries far from Egypt's sphere of influence. The most likely place for these would have been around the North Atlantic coast of Brittany.

In ancient times, a criminal's punishment sometimes included having his tongue cut out; the tongue was often fed to the sovereign's pets. This is perhaps the origin of the question, 'Cat got your tongue?'

The fate of the cat in Europe changed radically during the Middle Ages, when it became an object of superstition and associated with evil. For those people who were suspected of practising witchcraft, ownership of cats would often serve as proof and both cat and owner would be put to death. With the cat population dwindling, the numbers of disease-carrying rats increased, a factor that contributed greatly to the spread of plagues and other epidemics throughout Europe.

By the seventeenth century the cat had begun to regain its former place as a companion to people and as a pest controller. Many writers, particularly in France and England, began to keep cats as pets and to write about their good qualities. It became fashionable to own and breed cats, especially the long-haired varieties. By the late 1800s, cat exhibitions were being held in Britain and the United States, and cat fanciers' organizations were established.

It is not clear when cats were first introduced to America. Anecdotal evidence suggests that cats were brought over by the pilgrims on the *Mayflower*.

In 1868 the 'Cat System' was introduced in London, whereby three cats were employed as mousers in public buildings, at a salary of two shillings (24d; 10p) per week.

The first breeding pair of Siamese cats arrived in England in 1884.

The first formal cat show was held in England in 1871; in America, in 1895.

NINE LIVES

The origin of the belief that a cat has 'nine lives' is unknown. One possibility is that the number 9 is the 'trinity of trinities' and therefore considered lucky.

Their extreme physical flexibility and suppleness have meant that cats are often able to survive high falls, which may have contributed to the belief that they frequently appear to cheat death, and thus have more than one life.

Witches were sometimes said to have the ability to shape-shift into a cat a total of nine times, which may account for their familiars being said to have nine lives.

THE BLACK CAT

The black cat has been associated with evil since pre-Christian times. Hebrew and Babylonian folklore, for example, compared the cat to a coiled serpent – the association is perhaps unlikely until one considers a cat's favourite position, curled up by a hearth or fire. However, it was in Europe during the Middle Ages that these cats became synonymous with witches, witchcraft, black magic and bad luck. More recently, the black cat has been both a symbol of the Wicca religion, and of some anarchist political parties. However, in certain countries, black cats are considered lucky, and white cats are the harbingers of bad luck. Some black cat superstitions:

* If a black cat crosses your path, quickly look up to the sky and before you return home from your journey you may find some money.

* If a black cat visits your house, then good fortune will visit you – the blacker the luckier!

* If you meet a black cat while travelling along the street, you should return home and begin your journey again, otherwise you will find bad luck.

* If a black cat starts to cross your path but turns back halfway, you will have bad luck. However, the cat that continues across your path will bring you good luck.

Cats' Blood

Cats have three blood types: A, B and AB. The majority are type A.

Cat blood is transferable to other cats in the same way that humans can donate blood to one another. An animal hospital in New Jersey, USA, even appointed an official blood donor, by the name of Fat Albert, to provide much-needed blood transfusions for injured cats.

Each Nation to its Own
– Cat Superstitions

If you hear a cat sneeze, it is a good omen – Italy.

A black cat on your porch brings prosperity – Scotland.

When moving to a new home, always put the cat through a window first instead of the door, so that it will not leave – USA.

If you find one white hair on a black cat
then you will be lucky – France.

On seeing a one-eyed cat you should spit on your thumb,
and press your thumb into the palm of your hand.
Now, if you make a wish, it will come true – USA.

Cats should not be allowed into a room where a private family
discussion is taking place, as the cat will spread gossip around
the town – the Netherlands.

Seeing a tortoiseshell cat foretells death by accident –
Normandy, France.

It is lucky to own a black cat, but unlucky to come
across one by chance – Yorkshire, England.

Don't cross a stream carrying a cat;
it's bad luck – France.

MORE LORE – CATS AND THE WEATHER

It has been said that cats can forecast the weather – expect high winds when a cat claws at the carpet or at curtains, and rain when a cat washes its ears. A particularly abundant source of such lore comes from the maritime world; sailors were generally a superstitious group and their belief in cats' possession of other-worldly powers made them a useful barometer of the weather and an oracle on the outcome of a voyage. Cats that cried or mewed loudly would signify a difficult voyage, while a playful cat reassured sailors that the wind would blow in their favour and their journey would be a swift one. English sailors will still say a cat 'has a gale of wind in her tail' if it is unusually frisky.

In the Harz Mountains, in northern Germany, the stormy north-west wind is known as 'the Cat's Nose'.

In Indonesia, cats were thought to control the rain. To summon rain, water is poured on a cat. Even today, the Korat breed of cat, a native of Thailand, is sometimes ceremonially sprinkled with water to bring rain for the crops.

In the UK, a cat sleeping with all four paws tucked under its body means cold weather is approaching.

RECORD-BREAKING CATS

These remarkable records have been verified from several sources and are correct at the time of writing.

A record exists for the cat with the most toes! Jake, who lives in Ontario, Canada, has twenty-eight toes – seven on each paw, as counted on September 2002. Each toe has its own bone structure, claw and pad. The previous record in this category was held by Mickey, a tabby from New York, USA, who had twenty-seven digits.

The oldest cat on record to give birth was Litty, who, in 1987 and at the age of thirty, had two kittens.

The eccentrically named Tarawood Antigone, a female Burmese who lived in England, currently holds the record for producing the largest litter in recorded history. In August 1970, when the mother was four years old, she gave birth by Caesarean section to nineteen kittens, consisting of one female, fourteen males and four stillborn.

The world's longest domestic cat lives in Illinois, Chicago. His name is Leo, his breed is Maine Coon, and he measures 48 inches (122 centimetres) from his nose to the tip of his tail.

The smallest cat on record is a male blue-point Himalayan Persian called Tinker Toy. Tinker Toy was a diminutive 2.75 inches (7 centimetres) tall and just 7.5 inches (19 centimetres) long when fully grown. This tiny feline lived in Illinois, USA.

Mr Peebles from the United States held the record for the lightest fully grown cat, weighing only 3 pounds (1.4 kilograms) even when he was two years old.

A cat named Blackie is recorded as the richest cat, when his owner, millionaire Ben Rea, left him over $20 million in his will.

He died in April 1998, and shortly after was confirmed as the world's oldest cat – Granpa Rex lived to the ripe old age of thirty-four years, two months and four hours. The previous record holder was a female tabby from Devon, England, called Ma, who died in 1957 aged thirty-four years and one day.

The heaviest cat was a real monster – an Australian cat named Himmy weighed 45 pounds, 10 ounces (approximately 20.5 kilograms).

An American cat named Furball is credited with having the longest tail. In March 2001, Furball's tail measured 16 inches (40.6 centimetres).

The greatest height on record from which a cat has fallen and survived is sixteen storeys. Andy, the cat in question, was the pet of Florida senator Ken Myer.

Smarty holds the world record for the greatest number of flights made by a cat. As of May 2002, he had made sixty-four flights, all of them between Cyprus and Egypt, where his owners live.

CATS' NOSES

Cats have a special scent organ located in the roof of their mouths called the vomeronasal organ, or Jacobson's organ, with which it analyses odours. Snakes also possess this organ.

A cat has approximately 60 to 80 million olfactory (smell) cells – humans have no more than 20 million.

A cat's nose is variously called a 'nose pad', or 'nose leather'.

Like human fingerprints, each feline 'noseprint' is completely unique.

A cat's nose leather may be black, reddish, or pink and is usually cool and moist.

Although a kitten is born blind, touch receptors in its nose have already developed, and this sense is used by the kitten to make contact with the mother. Nose-touching remains a friendly greeting between cats throughout their lives.

SOME PLANTS POISONOUS TO CATS – 3

Delphinium
Devil's Ivy
Dumb Cane
Eggplant
Elderberry
Elephant Ears
Eucalyptus
False acacia
Ferns

Flax
Foxglove
Gaultheria
Geranium
Giant Hogweed
Hellebore
Hemlock
Henbane
Holly

Honeysuckle
Horse chestnut
Hyacinth
Hydrangea
Impatiens
Ivy
Lace Fern

Lilies – all lilies are toxic to cats, including arum and tiger lilies, and lily of the valley. The *Liliaceae* family contains many plants that do not immediately seem to be obvious relations of the lily, including bluebells, hyacinths and tulips, as well as other related plants like amaryllis, daffodils and jonquils.

MISCELLANEOUS CAT FACTS

* A person who loves cats is called an ailurophile; cat haters are known as ailurophobes. This stems from the classical Greek word for cat, *ailouros*.

* The domestic cat belongs to the species *Felis domesticus*.

* A group of kittens is called a kindle.

✳ When a domestic cat goes after mice, each pounce in three results in a catch.

✳ A group of adult cats is called a clowder.

✳ One man made a fortune from the invention of cat litter – Edward Lowe. First manufactured in 1947, the granulated clay was originally designed to help out a neighbour who was complaining about the mess as a result of using ashes in her cat's tray. He sold his business in 1990 for approximately US $200 million (£110 million).

✳ *Gay Purr-ee*, released in 1962, was the first full-length film to feature a cat as the star. Mewsette, the cat in question, was voiced by Judy Garland.

✳ Recent research reveals what all cat lovers already know – that owning a cat may be good for your health. The studies seem to suggest that cat owners suffer from fewer minor health problems and have lower blood pressure and cholesterol levels. Stroking a cat seems to calm an individual and relieve stress.

✳ The life expectancy of cats has nearly doubled since 1930 – from eight to sixteen years.

Everlasting Cats

A company in Utah in the US will mummify your cat. Summum Modern Mummifications can mummify cats and also embalm humans, and they use a patented technique that is derived from ancient Egyptian methods. To have your cat mummified will cost around $4,500 (approximately £2,500).

The first cat cloned to order was sold in the USA in 2004. The cat, Nicky, cost $49,680 (£26,000) and was cloned from a seventeen-year-old cat who had died the year before. The owner had 'banked' her cat's DNA, and this was used to create the clone. The owner claims the 'new' Nicky is identical to his predecessor.

Cat Ages

Cat Age	Human Age
6 months	10 years
8 months	13 years
1 year	15 years
2 years	24 years
4 years	32 years
6 years	40 years
8 years	48 years
10 years	56 years
12 years	64 years
14 years	72 years
16 years	80 years
18 years	88 years
20 years	96 years
21 years	100 years

CATS AND COMPUTERS

Do not allow long-haired black cats to sleep atop laser printers and tape drives. The black hair is almost invisible in black patterns, gears, and rollers. – JEFF LIEBERMANN

Do not meddle in the affairs of cats, for they are subtle and they will pee on your computer. – BRUCE GRAHAM

A computer and a cat are somewhat alike: they both purr, and like to be stroked, and spend a lot of the day motionless. They also have secrets they don't necessarily share.
JOHN UPDIKE

HOW TO BEFRIEND A CAT

Cats are picky companions, and it's not always easy to make friends with a cat. It has to be on their terms.

Of all the steps towards winning a cat's approval, perhaps the most important is not to try too hard. Be gentle in your approach and with your touch; don't stroke them vigorously or try to pick

them up. If the cat moves towards you and rubs against your leg, then you have passed the first stage of approval.

Once you've achieved this approval, hold your hand steady about a foot or so from the cat's face, and if it pushes its cheek against your fingers, then that's the second stage completed. Don't force the cat if it appears unsure or reluctant – remember, it all has to be the cat's idea.

It's also important to keep your voice even and unthreatening. If you have a deep voice, try raising the pitch a little – cats sometimes equate a low voice with their enemies. And finally, remember that cats are incredibly territorial, so don't threaten their space.

FAMOUS CAT OWNERS – 3

Nostradamus (1503–66) The French physician and astrologer Michel de Notre-Dame, more usually known by the Latin form of his surname, Nostradamus, under which he published his collection of predictions known as *Centuries*, had a cat named Grimalkin. The archaic English word 'grimalkin', meaning a cat, dates from the late sixteenth century, and is a combination of 'grey' and 'Malkin', a pet form of the name Matilda.

Edgar Allan Poe (1809–1849) The American poet, critic and short-story writer Edgar Allan Poe loved cats and kept several, despite a complicated and often stormy personal life, made worse by poverty and alcoholism. His admiration for cats, however, did not stop him from portraying them as sinister portents or familiars, or even as nemesis, in several of his horror stories. He used his tortoiseshell cat, Catarina as the inspiration for one of his darkest tales, 'The Black Cat'. This seems rather unfair to the loyal Catarina, for in the winter of 1846, when Poe was destitute and his wife lay close to death from tuberculosis, the cat would warm the dying woman by curling up on the bed alongside her.

Cardinal Richelieu (1585–1642) Armand Jean du Plessis, Cardinal and duc de Richelieu, was one of the greatest French statesmen, and, as Minister of State to King Louis XIII (effectively, prime minister) from 1624, one of the most powerful men in the Europe of his day. Yet although Richelieu pursued witches with almost fanatical zeal, he did not share the pervading ignorance about, and suspicion of, cats, which was based on the medieval superstition that the animals served as witches' 'familiars'. Indeed, at the time of his death he owned fourteen cats, and engaged two maids to feed them foie gras – then, as now, an expensive delicacy – twice a day; he is even said to have dined with the animals sometimes. One of his last requests as he lay dying was for the cats and their two attendants to be provided with a house and an allowance. Richelieu's cats were:

Felimare – a tabby who looked like a tiger
Gazette – the most indiscreet. A gazette is a kind of newspaper; to call someone *une vraie gazette* is to say that they know all the local gossip

Lucifer – a jet-black Angora, saviour of many witches' cats (see page 68)

Ludovic le Cruel – the best hunter and ratter

Ludoviska – a Polish cat

Mimi-Paillon – another Angora

Mounard le Fougueux – of a somewhat erratic and irritable nature (*mounard* means fiery or spirited)

Perruque – a French word for a wig'; Racan's sibling (see below)

Pyrame and **Thisbe** – named after the famous lovers of classical legend (in English, Pyramus and Thisbe), for the two cats often curled together to sleep

Racan – the name of a scholar in whose wig the cat was born

Rubis sur l'Ongle – literally, 'ruby on the [finger]nail', a French expression meaning to pay cash on the nail. A very neat cat with a passion for milk

Serpolet – a sun lover. *Serpolet* is the French word for wild thyme

Soumise – the Cardinal's favourite. *Soumise* means docile, submissive, obedient

Domenico Scarlatti (1685–1757) The Italian virtuoso harpsichordist and composer Domenico Scarlatti owned a cat called Pulcinella, named after a character in commedia dell'arte (an improvised kind of popular comedy based on stock characters) who speaks in Neapolitan dialect, has an enormous nose and is always hungry. Scarlatti's Pulcinella would jump up on to the keyboard of his harpsichord and walk up and down on the keys. Eventually he composed a fugue based upon the cat's antics, which became known as 'The Cat's Fugue' (properly, Fugue in G minor, K30; L499).

Much the same behaviour by a cat is said to have led Frédéric Chopin to compose his Waltz for Piano in F major, Op. 34/3 (CT 209), better known as 'The Cat's Waltz'. Meanwhile, composers

such as Gioacchino Rossini and Maurice Ravel also paid homage to cats, the former with his *Duetto buffo di due gatti* (Comic Duet for Two Cats, but usually just known as 'The Cat Duet'), and the latter with a cat-themed opera, *L'Enfant et les sortilèges* ('the child and the spells', but generally known as *The Bewitched Child*), based on a story by Colette (see page 24). There is a cat represented by a recurring theme on the clarinet in Sergei Prokofiev's 'children's piece', *Peter and the Wolf*, and Prokofiev also wrote a dance for a cat into his ballet *Cinderella*. Many other composers have written incidental music either about or inspired by cats, among them the great twentieth-century American composer Aaron Copland (1900–90).

Some Symptoms of a Poisoned Cat

If you suspect that a cat has been poisoned, warning signs include collapsing, repeated vomiting, excessive skin irritation, drooling, convulsions, or severe diarrhoea. Similarly, if a cat is lethargic and off its food, something could be wrong. Do not attempt to make the cat regurgitate what it has swallowed, and get your cat to a vet as soon as you suspect poisoning. A sample of the plant, if possible, will help with identification. Never give a cat human painkillers, such as paracetamol, as these can be fatal for cats.

FAMOUS AILUROPHOBES

Julius Caesar, King Henri II of France, King Charles XI of Sweden, Mussolini and Genghis Khan were all said to have hated cats. Hitler is known to have despised cats, and Napoleon Bonaparte was terrified of them. The French Emperor was once heard calling out in fear from his bedroom, only to be found sweating profusely and wielding his sword at a tiny kitten.

CATS IN ART

The history of the depiction of cats in art is almost as old as art itself. The domesticated cat has been a favourite subject of artists and writers since prehistoric times, while the wild animal, and especially big cats, have also fascinated many artists over the centuries. Representations of cats survive in fragments, and sometimes larger survivals, from ancient Greece, Crete, Babylon, Rome, Egypt and many other civilizations; indeed, some of the oldest artistic depictions are the ancient sculptures and drawings of the Egyptian cat goddess Bastet found in the Nile Valley.

The cat was also frequently portrayed in ancient Japan, where some of the drawings were so realistic that they were thought to have magical powers. People believed that if the drawings themselves were hung in homes and in temples they kept rats and mice away. Japanese Buddhists venerate cats after death, and the temple of Go-To-Ku-Ji in Tokyo is dedicated to them. In each of the sculptures, relief carvings and paintings adorning the temple, the cat has a paw raised as if in greeting, a classical pose believed to bring good luck. Other Eastern civilizations, notably those of China and India, produced art that included cats, both as incidental subjects, and in straightforward depictions, while many Western artistic works from at least the Middle Ages, not just paintings and carvings but also tapestries such as *La Dame au Licorne* and illustrated religious works that emanated from monasteries before the coming of the printing press, include cats either figuratively or symbolically, and often as 'accessories' for the subjects of portraiture. A list of Western artists since the sixteenth century who have included depictions of cats in their works would be enormously long; it would include Leonardo, Rembrandt, Vandyke, Gainsborough, Van Gogh, Renoir, Morisot, Toulouse-Lautrec, Modigliani, Chagall, Klee, Rousseau and Picasso. There have been, too, artists who have made a name for themselves as painters of cats, among them Théophile-Alexandre Steinlen (see page 95) and Louis Wain (see page 120).

Paul Klee (1879–1940) The Swiss artist Paul Klee depicted a wide-eyed, watchful cat in his popular painting *Cat and Bird*. The simple image shows the bird on the cat's forehead, literally on his mind, fulfilling the artist's desire to 'make secret visions visible'.

Leonardo da Vinci (1452–1519) The Florentine painter, sculptor, architect, musician, engineer, scientist and thinker, perhaps the greatest genius of the Italian Renaissance, said of cats, 'the smallest feline is a masterpiece.' Only some thirteen paintings by Leonardo are known to survive, but he did make studies for a painting entitled *The Madonna with the Cat*, although whether he never completed it, or whether the finished work has been lost or destroyed, is not known. The initial studies, however, are in the

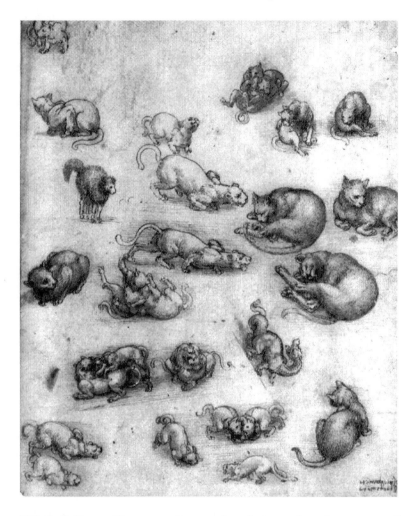

Uffizi Gallery, Florence. Leonardo also produced a page of sketches of cats, detailing their movements and positions; amusingly, the page of drawings also includes a sketch of a dragon.

Pablo Picasso (1881–1973) Like Paul Klee, the Spanish painter Pablo Picasso also produced a work entitled *Cat and Bird*. In the latter's work, however, the depiction of the cat attacking the bird is allegorical of the cruelty of General Franco's Fascist government in Spain.

Pierre Auguste Renoir (1841–1919) The French Impressionist artist loved cats and depicted them in several paintings. Some of the best known are *Portrait of Madame Manet, Julie Manet with a Cat* and *Sleeping Girl with a Cat*.

Marc Chagall (1887–1985) The Russian-born French painter Marc Chagall often depicted cats with very human faces and vice versa, as can be seen in his coloured etching of *circa* 1928–31, *The Cat Transformed Into a Woman*.

Rembrandt (1606–69) The Dutch painter and etcher Rembrandt Harmenszoon van Rijn was the greatest northern European artist of his age. In his etching *The Virgin and Child with Cat*, Rembrandt uses the presence of the cat, within a domestic setting, to convey a feeling of intimacy in his depiction of the Nativity.

Théophile-Alexandre Steinlen (1859–1923) The Swiss-born French art-nouveau painter and printmaker was famous for his advertising posters, in which he frequently depicted cats. He drew upon his home life for inspiration – his house in Paris was known as 'Cats' Corner' – and would often incorporate his family and their cats in his works. His cats are sometimes elegantly realistic, and sometimes more stylized, but his work shows a deep understanding of the animals. Among his most famous advertisements featuring cats are *Tournée du Chat Noir* (1896; Le Chat Noir was a Parisian cabaret) and *Lait Pur Stérilisé* (1894).

Fat Cat – How to Tell
if Your Cat is Overweight

The average weight for an adult cat is between 100 and 180 ounces (3 and 5 kilograms) – some cats have bigger bones than others.

In order to tell if a cat is overweight, look at it from above and slowly run your fingers over its sides, from its shoulders to its tail.

If you can see and feel its ribs easily, then it is underweight.

If you can't see a cat's ribs but can feel them when you press your fingers lightly on its flanks, then it is the correct weight. You will also see a slight indentation just behind its ribs when you look at your cat from above.

If you have difficulty feeling its ribs and it's difficult to make out this indentation then your cat is almost certainly overweight.

If you can't feel its ribs or this indentation at all then it is likely to be obese. Overweight cats also behave differently – they walk slowly and are reluctant to play.

CATS IN ANCIENT EGYPT

The ancient Egyptian word for cat was *mau*, which means 'to see'.

About five thousand years ago, cats were accepted members of the households of Egypt; indeed, the Egyptians were the first civilization to tame the cat. Many of the breeds we know today have evolved from these ancient cats. For the Egyptians, however, the cat was more than just a pet; they were used to hunt fish and birds, and to keep down the rat and mice populations that infested the grain stocks along the Nile.

Egyptians considered the cat so valuable that laws were created to protect it, and this reverence of the feline developed into a cult of cat worship that would last for more than two thousand years. To kill a cat was a crime punishable by death.

The Egyptians also had strict laws prohibiting the export of their cats, but their value as rat-catchers meant that cats were taken by the Greeks and Romans to most parts of Europe. Domestic cats could also be found in India, China and Japan, where they were prized as pets as well as rodent catchers.

Sacred cats were kept in sanctuaries in ancient Egypt, and carefully tended to by priests who watched them day and night. The priests made their famous predictions by interpreting even the smallest movement of the cats; a purr or even twitch of a whisker may have been observed and noted. The temple cats wore heavily jewelled collars, and were treated like royalty. The cat goddess, Bastet, became one of the most sacred figures of worship. She was represented as having the head of a cat.

Cats were said to be able to control the moon's movement and to protect the dead, and were given total authority over the royal houses at night because of their ability to see in the dark.

When a cat belonging to an ancient Egyptian family died, the entire household would remove their eyebrows as a sign of mourning.

After a cat's death, its body was mummified and buried in a special cemetery alongside embalmed mice, which the cat could eat in the afterlife. In the excavated remains of one temple, uncovered in the nineteenth century, the preserved bodies of more than 300,000 cats were discovered.

A Few Cat Dangers

Remember to cat-proof your home – keep out of 'reach' any materials that may look enticing to play with, but which will cause harm if swallowed, such as elastic bands, paper clips and untied string.

A cat's paws can absorb chemicals that are used on floors. Floor waxes and cleaning solutions pose a particular danger.

Keep aerosol sprays away from a cat and its food, as they too contain dangerous chemicals.

Being shiny and easy to play with, coins are a particular hazard for a cat, so make sure they are not left lying around.

Cats in Advertising

Unsurprisingly, cats have often been used in advertising to promote products designed for their use, a famous example being Morris the Cat and 9Lives cat food in the USA (see page 64), or, some years ago, another 'celebrity' cat, Arthur, a white cat that ate

with his paw, promoting Whiskas cat food in the UK. Cats have, however, also been used since the early days of organized advertising to promote an enormous number of other products aimed at the human market. Depictions of pet cats, for instance, are often used to convey an idea of comfort and domesticity, while big cats like lions suggest strength and power or, as with leopards and cheetahs, speed, grace and beauty.

In America and Continental Europe a black cat is normally considered to be a harbinger of bad luck; in Britain, however, it is regarded as a good-luck symbol. For this reason, the tobacco concern Carreras introduced in 1904 a brand of cigarettes called Black Cat, printing an image of a black cat on the packaging and in its advertisements in the hope that people would associate the brand with good luck. Black Cat cigarettes disappeared from the marketplace towards the end of the twentieth century. Another brand from Carreras, the cork-tipped, filterless Craven 'A' cigarettes (now long defunct in that form), also featured the head of a black cat on the packaging.

In the USA in 1984 there was even a book published with the title *The Cat Made Me Buy It: A Collection of Cats Who Sold Yesterday's Products*.

CATS AND MUSIC

It appears that feline taste in music is as varied as it is in humans. Some cats show no interest in it, while others clearly adore it. A study conducted in the 1930s by Dr Morin and Dr Bachrach made

the surprising discovery that the note E of the fourth octave made young cats defecate and adult cats become sexually excited.

Extremely high notes can cause agitation in many cats, and it would appear that such confusion and distress occurs because the sounds are similar to some of the 'words' in the feline vocabulary. Some of the high notes, for example, may approximate the pitch of the mews of a distressed kitten and therefore may disturb an adult cat, especially a female. An erotic response may be due to the similarity of the tones to the sounds made during the feline courtship ritual. In other words, be careful what music you play around your cat!

CATS' MOUTHS

A full feline dental set contains thirty teeth (twelve incisors, ten premolars, four canine and four molar teeth). Like humans, kittens too have baby teeth, which are replaced by permanent teeth approximately seven months after birth.

The tiny backward-facing barbs on a cat's tongue – which account for its rough feeling – scoop water backwards into the mouth when the cat drinks. These 'hooks' are called papillae.

A simple hinge connects a cat's upper and lower jaws but this arrangement only allows for an up-and-down motion. A cat cannot move its lower jaw sideways, nor can it grind its teeth. In consequence, cats eat by tearing and crushing their food, but they do not chew it; digestive juices in the stomach help to break down food that is swallowed whole.

Like humans, cats are subject to gum disease and to dental decay. Ideally, a cat dentist or vet should clean a cat's teeth once every year.

BELIEVE IT OR NOT

* Cats have no sweat glands, and therefore never sweat.

* Cat racing was once a spectator sport in England, though it wasn't particularly popular. The first official cat racetrack opened in Dorset in 1936, and took a form very similar to that of greyhound racing, with a number of cats chasing an electric mouse round a track. For one reason or another, however, it never captured the public imagination, and the last official track closed in 1949.

* Cats are renowned for their ability to survive falls from great heights. However, studies have shown that a cat falling from a height equivalent to eight storeys have a greater chance of sustaining fewer injuries, and of survival,

than a cat that falls from a lesser height. The theory states that once a cat has reached terminal velocity (after falling approximately the height of five storeys) it will spread its limbs and instinctively relax, and thus better absorb the impact of the fall when it hits the ground.

* Dogs are not the only domesticated animals with a monopoly on loyalty to their owners above and beyond the call of duty. Stories abound of cats who have stayed by their injured owners, calling and screeching until help has arrived, or alerting family members during house fires.

Inventions for Cats

As cat lovers know, felines are not fond of hot food. This knowledge has been taken to the extreme in Japan, where people often share tidbits of their supper with their pets. Here, a person who blows on their food before eating is described as having a 'cat's tongue'. 'Food Temperature Control for Cats' is a 'Chindogu' invention (*chindogu* is a Japanese word meaning 'weird tool', and is a general name for an odd or useless invention) which enables a cat to cool its own food by operating with its paw a small pump which blows cold air on to their meal.

Another Chindogu invention is a set of duster slippers for cats, with which one's cat can help out with the household dusting just by walking around the house.

In 2000, Chris Niswander, a computer programmer from Tucson, won an Ig Nobel Prize (an award celebrating unusual, and, ideally, unrepeatable achievements in a wide range of fields) for his computer program *PawSense*. The software detects when your cat is playing havoc on your computer by walking over the keys, and sounds an alarm to scare the trespasser away.

CATS' TAILS

A cat's tail is used primarily to maintain balance, and it contains almost 10 per cent of the total number of bones in its body.

The domestic cat is the only species of cat able to hold its tail up vertical while walking.

When a cat winds its tail around something or someone, it is a sign of affection.

The tail plays a vital role in the 'righting reflex', the instinctive ability that allows a cat to rotate whilst falling and enabling it to land on its feet.

Something of a cat's mood can be read in its tail. A tail held high shows happiness, while a twitching tail is a warning sign, and a tail tucked close to the body is sign of insecurity or fear.

A Great Mouser

A female tortoiseshell called Towser (1963–87) holds the record as the champion mouser of all time. She was owned by and lived in the Glenturret distillery in Scotland, where she is reported to have killed an average of three mice a day every day of her adult life, giving an estimated total of almost thirty thousand kills.

Cats and Birds

Cats are often blamed for the diminishing population of birds in the wild. However, while domestic and feral cats can certainly be bird-hunters, most research shows that cats are not the primary killers of wild birds. The domestic outdoor cat's diet is similar to that of its ancestor, the African wild cat, and its close relative, the European wild cat, with mice making up 75 per cent of the diet, birds 15 per cent, and reptiles around 10 per cent. In fact, wild animals take a greater toll on birdlife than cats do. Humans are a bird's worst enemy, however, with our destruction of their habitat, use of pesticides, and air pollution, all of which kill vast numbers of birds every year.

The truth is . . . cats will go after whatever is easiest to catch, whether that is birds, mice, frogs or insects. The cat's hunting style is best suited to catching rodents, not birds. To really cramp a cat's style, add a bell to its collar.

Cats' Incredible Journeys – 2

Kuzya, a pet moggy in Russia, embarked on a 1,300-mile (2,100-kilometre) trek across Siberia to be reunited with his owners. Kuzya ran away from his family while they were all travelling on holiday. After weeks of desperate searching they decided he was dead and returned home – three months later, Kuzya turned up on their doorstep in perfect health.

The fantastically named cat Princess Truman Tai-Tai travelled over 1.5 million miles (more than 2.4 million kilometres) during her sixteen-year employment on the British ship *Sagamire*.

A black-and-white cat named Tom had to be collected from Heathrow by his owner after he got lost in the hold of a British Airways aeroplane for two months. During this time he travelled more than half a million miles (approximately 800,000 kilometres) and visited several continents.

Hamlet escaped from his cage on a flight from Toronto, Canada, and travelled 600,000 miles (965,000 kilometres) until his rescue seven months later.

What to do in a Cat Emergency

In the unlikely event of a cat emergency, a few simple pointers will better prepare you to handle the situation.

For burns and scalds, act immediately, and sponge the affected area with cold water. For chemical burns, clean away any remaining residue, and then take your cat to the vet.

Cats can sometimes suffer from their encounters with bees and wasps. If stung by bee, remove the sting from the cat with tweezers and bathe the area with a solution of baking soda. With wasp stings, simply clean the sting area with diluted vinegar.

Cats at War

A black-and-white cat, later named Adolf, travelled a total of over 90,000 miles (144,000 kilometres) with the US Fifth Air Force that fought in the Pacific theatre in the Second World War. He first climbed aboard a cargo plane in Darwin, Australia, in 1945,

and developed the habit of hiding among the radio apparatus and appearing just as the engines started.

Wing Commander Guy Gibson, VC, the famous 'dambuster' of the Second World War, was often accompanied on his dangerous missions by his pet cat, Windy, 'an all-swimming, all-flying cat' who put in more flying hours than many pilots.

Known as the 'Animals' VC', the Dickin Medal was instituted in 1943 and is awarded to animals for 'conspicuous gallantry and devotion to duty' while serving with Britain's armed forces or civil-defence units. Since then it has been awarded to three horses, thirty-two pigeons, twenty dogs (most recently during the Iraq conflict in December 2003) – and one cat. This was Simon, the mascot of the British frigate HMS *Amethyst* during the Yangtze Incident in 1949, and who, though badly wounded by the blast from a Chinese Communist shell, stayed at his post and continued to kill rats throughout the ship's 101-day ordeal. Twenty-three of the *Amethyst*'s crew, including her captain, died. Simon survived to return to Britain with the ship after her epic escape down river, but died of his wounds a month later. In 1993,

Simon's Dickin Medal was sold at auction for more than £23,000 (US $42,000).

During the First World War some 500,000 cats were officially employed by British forces to serve as ratters and mousers in the trenches. They also alerted troops to the advance of poisonous gas clouds, saving thousands of lives.

Cats deployed to hunt vermin in food stores during the Second World War were considered so important that they were awarded a powdered milk ration in honour of their service. The United States later launched a 'Cats for Europe' campaign and shipped thousands of American cats to France for similar purposes.

A Pennsylvanian family was reported to have sent a black cat to England, which was then flown to Europe, with the intention that he would cross Hitler's path and bring him bad luck.

A female tabby named Faith and her kitten, Panda, made headlines in London newspapers during the Blitz when they were discovered under the debris of St Augustine's Church after it suffered a direct hit from a bomb. The pair had been hiding in a storage cubby-hole in the rectory basement following heavy bombing in the preceding few days. Faith was awarded a silver medal and a certificate to celebrate her 'steadfast courage in the battle of London'.

When US Sergeant Rick Bousfield learned his unit was leaving Iraq, he refused to leave a certain member of his team behind. He sought help from the Alley Cat Allies, a non-profit organization that raises awareness about the plight of feral cats, and attempts to place them in loving homes. To assist Rick, the organization raised money for vaccinations, official papers and a plane ticket to get home safely the tabby cat that had joined his team during their service. The cat became acquainted with the soldiers after it caught five mice in the mess hall; he was adopted, and named 'Hammer', after their unit. Soldiers frequently tucked Hammer into their body armour during artillery attacks, and he provided much-needed stress relief between combat. He now lives with Sergeant Bousfield in Denver, Colorado, USA.

CAT TRICKS

Instances of performing cats are rare, although a few cats have been trained for the circus. Similarly, cats have also appeared in films. While cats can be trained to perform tricks, unlike dogs they rarely respond to affectionate contact as a reward. As any cat owner will recognize, in these situations, using a favourite food is often a valuable tool to encourage the cat to follow instructions.

A good example of encouragement by stomach is in training a cat to jump over a stick. Begin by placing the stick on the ground and immediately rewarding the cat with food whenever it happens to walk over it. Before long, the cat should begin to walk over the

stick deliberately in order to receive its treat. Now, proceed gradually to raise the stick above the ground, until the cat performs an impressive leap. Once the cat has achieved this, stagger the treat-giving, so that food is only given after the third or fourth successful attempt at the trick. This will encourage persistence.

Similarly, cats can be encouraged to touch and eventually to pick up small items if these are – of course – first smeared with food to attract their attention.

Only positive reinforcement should be given, as scolding is likely to dissuade your cat from trying the 'trick' at all.

Cats tend to learn through observation and choice rather than simply accepting the will of their owners!

AMERICAN CAT LAWS

✗ In Idaho, it is illegal for a cat to intercede in a fight between two dogs.

✗ In Louisiana, cats are prohibited by law from chasing ducks in city streets.

✗ In Montana, cats are legally obliged to wear three bells as a warning to birds of their approach.

✗ In Dallas, cats are instructed by law to wear a headlight when wandering the streets after dark.

✗ In Natchez, Mississippi, it is illegal for cats to drink beer.

HOW TO TOILET TRAIN YOUR CAT

For those people inclined towards teaching their cat how to use the toilet, this may help.

The transition from litter tray to toilet is an incremental process, and may take time. Begin by ensuring the toilet seat is permanently up and the bathroom door is always open. Place the litter tray next to the toilet, and ensure that the cat is using the tray regularly and correctly. Then, gradually, raise the tray off the floor by placing newspapers or boxes beneath it. Aim to raise it about two inches a day.

Over time, this process will familiarize the cat with having to jump to reach the tray, and eventually the cat will use the toilet bowl as a stepping stone. At this stage, place the litter tray on the toilet seat. After a couple of days, remove the tray and replace it with a metal bowl, placed in the toilet, and into which litter is placed.

At this stage, check the cat's posture when it is 'on the toilet', and particularly whether all four paws are on the seat – they shouldn't be in the toilet bowl. The final stage is gradually to reduce the litter in the metal bowl, and eventually replace it with water. Once the cat has grown familiar with the water, take the bowl away.

Teaching a cat to flush is the hard part.

GREAT HEIGHTS

In September 1950, a group of climbers were followed to a height of over 14,000 feet (4,300 metres) on their ascent to the top of the Matterhorn in the Alps by a four-month-old kitten.

In 1928, a cat was found in a hut belonging to a mountaineering club, 9,000 feet (2,800 metres) above sea level in the Swiss Alps. It was then adopted by the hut's caretaker, and would often follow climbers to heights of over 12,000 feet (3,700 metres).

A cat named Zizou was adopted by a mountaineering club at Mont Blanc in the French Alps, in 1962, and often followed mountaineers up the slopes to the peak. The Albert Premier retreat where Zizou resided stands at almost 9,000 feet (2,800 metres) and the peak is over 15,000 feet (4,600 metres) above sea level.

A CAT HOTEL

The first recorded 'cat hotel' was established in Philadelphia, Pennsylvania, USA, and could accommodate one hundred cats in rooms that contained three storeys of shelves, each furnished with soft rugs. The lucky cats were also entitled to their own room and the attentions of a personal hairdresser, if desired. Meals – typically soup, cod, shrimps and mackerel served with milk or water – were served from plates at a dining table.

The World According to Cats

These are some of the rules that cats appear to live by:

* Do not allow there to be any closed doors in the house. To open doors, scratch and meow loudly. Once the door has been opened, walk away. A doorway at the front or back of a property is the ideal place to stop and collect one's thoughts. This is particularly important during very cold weather, rain or snow.

* If you feel the need to vomit, make a dash for the nearest chair. If you cannot get to a chair, an Oriental rug or shag-pile carpet will suffice.

* Computers provide many opportunities to be helpful. Jumping on keyboards, batting the cursor on the screen and lying in a human's lap to prevent their being able to type are all excellent ways of gaining your human's affection.

* Improve your owners' coordination skills by darting in front of them whenever possible, particularly on the stairs,

in the dark, or when they are carrying heavy objects or lots
of shopping.

* If offered a choice of humans with whom to spend your
  time, always choose the busiest, and offer them your
  assistance. If a human is reading, position yourself just
  between their eyes and the book. If they are reading a
  newspaper, jump on it. This will make a satisfying noise.
  Humans love to be startled.

* Occasionally, play a game of hide-and seek with your
  humans by concealing yourself in a place where they will
  not find you. Stay there for three to four hours. Once your
  humans start to panic, come out and they will reward you
  with affection and possibly treats.

SOME FAMOUS CAT OWNERS – 4

Dr Albert Schweitzer (1875–1965) Born in Alsace, Schweitzer became a philosopher, a musician (and authority on Bach), a theologian, and a medical missionary, and for his work in the latter field was awarded the Nobel Peace Prize in 1952. That he learned to be ambidextrous, however, Schweitzer owed to his cat Sizi. In 1913 Schweitzer had established a medical mission and hospital at Lambréné in French Equatorial Africa (now Gabon), to combat leprosy and sleeping sickness, endemic to the area. Sizi had a habit of falling asleep while lying on his arm, with the result that in order to continue writing the necessary prescriptions Schweitzer had to learn to use his other hand. Visitors to the clinic remarked upon his obvious love of the cat, as well as the way that he tended to indulge her.

Sir Walter Scott (1771–1832) The Scottish poet and novelist Sir Walter Scott, author, among many other works, of the Waverley Novels, which include *Rob Roy* and *Ivanhoe*, was devoted to cats, and owned a tabby, Hinx, which used to harass the writer's dogs. In the portrait of Scott by John Watson Gordon, the writer is seen at his desk with Hinx lying near by.

Patrick Stewart (1940–) Patrick Stewart, who played Jean-Luc Picard in the long-running *Star Trek* series, found his beloved cat

on the set of *Star Trek: The Next Generation*, the television series that ran from 1987 to 1994. He christened the animal Bella.

Harriet Beecher Stowe (1811–1896) The American writer Harriet Beecher Stowe enjoyed enormous success when her first serious work, the anti-slavery novel *Uncle Tom's Cabin*, was published, first in serial form in 1851–2, and then as a book in 1852. The novel did much to advance the anti-slavery cause in the North in the years immediately before the outbreak of the 'War Between the States', and Harriet found herself lionized not only among her Northern compatriots, but also in Britain, which she visited in 1853, 1856 and 1859, and where she was honoured by Queen Victoria. An indomitable figure of deep religiosity, Harriet met her match in Calvin, a Maltese cat who turned up on her doorstep one day. A gourmand of impressive size and bulk, Calvin took over the house, which he dominated with his insatiable appetite for food and an unquestioning belief that the household revolved around him. None the less, Harriet liked having Calvin around the place, and he would often sit on her shoulder while she was writing.

Carl van Vechten (1880–1964) The American novelist and music critic Carl van Vechten owned a female orange Persian cat called Ariel that had a number of unusual characteristics. Unlike most cats, she liked to retrieve objects, and would hide small objects such as keys, pens and scissors under a rug. Even more unusually for a cat, Ariel loved water and getting wet. She would jump of her own accord into the author's warm bath, or would sit in the washbasin under a running tap, enjoying the improvised shower.

Queen Victoria (1819–1901) Perhaps because of the loneliness of her long widowhood, the Queen Empress was extremely fond of cats. After she died, her cat, White Heather, continued to enjoy a comfortable, if not pampered, life in Buckingham Palace, living to a great age and dying during the reign of Victoria's eldest son and successor, King Edward VII. The Old Queen's reign, which lasted some sixty-four years, saw not only the highest point of British imperial power, but also an explosion in the popularity of cats as pets in Britain. Books and stories about cats started to appear, and the creatures began to feature, usually highly sentimentalized, in illustrations and on cards and packaging; the animals – kittens, as often as not – were frequently portrayed in a pretty if sentimental or trite way that came to be called 'chocolate-box'.

H. G. Wells (1866–1946) The English novelist and journalist Herbert George Wells was one of the early champions of the then new genre of science fiction, with books like *The Time Machine* (1895) and *The War of the Worlds* (1898). Unconventional, and occasionally scandalous, in his private life, the writer owned a cat named Mr Peter Wells, known to friends as Mr Peter. It is said that if the cat thought that one of Wells's guests was talking too much, or too loudly, he would get up from where he was sitting and ostentatiously make for the door.

OTHER CAT COLOURS

* It is considered very lucky to have a three-coloured cat come to your house.

* If a ginger cat crosses your path, you must immediately turn around and walk backwards to your destination in order to avert bad luck.

* The Russian Blue is considered a lucky breed in Russia, and consequently a new bride will sometimes be given a picture of such a cat.

* In Japan, a tortoiseshell-and-white cat is thought to be lucky.

IT'S A CAT'S WORLD – 3

One cat just leads to another. – ERNEST HEMINGWAY

Cats are rather delicate creatures and they are subject to a good many ailments, but I never heard of one who suffered from insomnia. – JOSEPH WOOD KRUTCH

Some people say that cats are sneaky, evil, and cruel.
True, and they have many other fine qualities as well.
MISSY DIZICK

We have a friend who hates cats. Every time he comes to
the house the cat sits on his knee. – Anonymous

A cat stretches from one end of my childhood to the other.
Blaga Dimitrova

All you have to remember is Rule 1: when in doubt, wash.
Paul Gallico

Cats always seem so very wise, when staring with their
half-closed eyes. Can they be thinking, I'll be nice, and maybe
she will feed me twice? – Bette Midler

Does the father figure in your cat's life ever clean the litter box?
My husband claims that men lack the scooping gene.
Barbara L. Diamond

Even overweight cats instinctively know the cardinal rule:
when fat, arrange yourself in slim poses. – John Weitz

I wonder what goes through his mind when he sees us
peeing in the water bowl. – Penny Ward Moser

Louis Wain

The English artist Louis Wain (1860–1939) was commonly known as 'the man who drew cats'. His style is incredibly distinctive, featuring anthropomorphized, large-eyed cats and kittens, often dressed up in human clothing, and taking part in human activities and pastimes. H. G. Wells, the English writer, said of Wain: 'He invented a cat style, a cat society, a whole cat world. English cats which do not look like Louis Wain cats are ashamed of themselves.'

Wain was a household name in nineteenth-century England. His popularity was such that it was said, 'Christmas without one of Louis's clever-catty pictures would be like Christmas pudding without currants.'

Perhaps Wain's inspiration came from his own black-and-white cat, Peter, a stray that became his favourite pet and nspiration.

When Louis was married in 1883, his sisters presented Peter to him and his new wife, Emily, as a wedding gift. Wain taught Peter some clever tricks, including holding his paws as if praying, wearing eyeglasses, and pretending to read.

His first commission came in 1886, resulting in 'A Kittens' Christmas', and his career as a cat illustrator was launched. He was also the President of the National Cat Club of England. He died in 1939 after suffering for some years with psychiatric illness, but his legacy – hundreds of fantastical and fanciful drawings of cats and kittens – lives on.

CAT NAMES

Cats respond most readily to names that end in an 'ee' sound.

SOME FEMALE CAT NAMES

Alice	Gigi	Mimi	Ruffles
Baby	Ginger	Minnie	Sadie
Betty	Gypsy	Missy	Taffy
Buffy	Iffy	Misty	Tammy
Cassie	Ivy	Mouse	Tibby
Cimmy	Jane	Pearl	Tiny
Cleo	Lily	Peggy	Tiva
Coco	Lolly	Perdy	Tweetie
Daisy	Lucie	Polly	
Ella	Lucky	Poppy	
Fay	Milly	Rosie	

Some Plants Poisonous to Cats – 4

Mistletoe
Oleander
Potato (shoots)
Primrose
Privet
Quercus
Rhododendron
Rhubarb
Rosary pea
Rubber plant
Sambucus
Skunk cabbage
Snowdrop

Spindle tree
Star of Bethlehem
Sweet pea
Tiger lily
Tobacco
Tomato plant (stem, leaves
    and green fruit)
Thornapple
Tulip
Umbrella Tree
Wisteria
Yew
Zebra plant

Chit C(h)at

ENGLISH	Cat	'Meow'	To purr
RUSSIAN	Kot / Koshka	'Miau'	Murlykat
PORTUGUESE	Gato	'Miau'	Roronar
TURKISH	Kedi	'Miau'	Mirlar
GREEK	Gata	'Mau'	Niaourizee
KOREAN	Koyangyi	'Yaong'	Grr Grrr
HUNGARIAN	Macska / Tita	'Miau'	Dormbol
NORWEGIAN	Katt	'Miau'	Myrreng
FINNISH	Kissa	'Mau'	Kehrää
HINDI	Billi	'Miau'	Billi ney awaaz ki = 'the cat is making a noise'
ITALIAN	Gatto	'Miau'	Fare le fusa
GERMAN	Katze	'Miau'	Schnurren
POLISH	Kot	'Miau'	Mruczec
FRENCH	Chat	'Miaou	Ronronner

Contrary Cats

Have you noticed how cats have the annoying habit of crying to be let out and then crying to be let back in again? This is because cats like to make brief surveys of their territory before returning to their comfortable position on the sofa. Humans often don't understand that cats like to make these inspection tours regularly but do not want to stay out very long unless there is something unusual going on.

How to Draw a Cat

A sitting cat, from behind, is just about manageable. Start with two circles, a smaller one above a larger one. Add ears, whiskers, neck and a tail.

If all else fails, draw paw-marks.

Cats in Trees

There has never been a skeleton of a cat found in a tree; therefore, they must come down on their own.

Old American saying

* Even though your cat may loudly proclaim the opposite, cats that can go up a tree can normally come down again on their own.

* Fire departments strongly advise opening a can of tuna, leaving the immediate area and waiting for the cat to grow hungry.

* In Great Britain, a cat has to be stuck in a tree for at least forty-eight hours before the fire brigade will come to the rescue.

Mincha

In the late 1940s, a black female cat named Mincha found herself stuck up a 40-foot (12-metre) tree in Buenos Aires, Argentina. She made it her home for the next six years of her life. During this time, she gave birth to three litters and was fed by locals who attached her meals to long poles.

TAIL PIECE